Ten Thousand Central Parks

TEN THOUSAND CENTRAL PARKS

A Climate-Change Parable

David Brown Morris

EMPIRE
STATE
EDITIONS

AN IMPRINT OF FORDHAM UNIVERSITY PRESS

NEW YORK 2026

Visit us online at www.fordhampress.com/empire-state-editions.

For EU safety / GPSR concerns: Mare Nostrum Group B.V., Mauritskade 21D, 1091 GC Amsterdam, The Netherlands, gpsr@mare-nostrum.co.uk

Library of Congress Cataloging-in-Publication Data available online at https://catalog.loc .gov.

Printed in the United States of America

28 27 26   5 4 3 2 1

First edition

For Margot

CONTENTS

2 + 2 doesn't make 4:
                              once it made 4 but
today nothing is known in this regard

—Nicanor Parra, *Antipoems* (2004)

INTRODUCTION

Why Central Park?

What is now proved was once, only imagin'd.
—William Blake, *The Marriage of Heaven and Hell* (1790)

Los Angeles is burning. Windswept apocalyptic firestorms whip across the hills and wipe out entire communities, nothing left but freestanding chimneys amid the debris, each chimney the remnant of a family, of broken lives. The unprecedented devastation erupting in January 2025 ranges from Pacific Palisades, where median home values soar into multimillions, to unincorporated Altadena in the foothills of the San Gabriel Mountains, where almost half the population is black or Latino and where 7.4 percent, according to the 2020 census, lives in poverty.[1] Along a half-mile strip of shoreline in Malibu, wall-to-wall compounds of the superrich lie in ruins, exposing a desolate seaside margin of smoldering ash, blackened girders, and—at 19010 Pacific Coast Highway—a surreal metal spiral staircase ascending into emptiness.[2] Drivers fleeing the inferno are trapped on gridlocked roadways, abandoning their cars.[3] The flames towering along iconic Sunset Boulevard leave a junkyard of trapped and burned-out automobiles, eventually pushed aside by bulldozers. "It's official," a respected journal announces in the sober language of fact: "2024 is the hottest year on record—and the first to exceed 1.5 degrees Celsius . . . above preindustrial temperatures." If mid-January in Los Angeles is any measure, the year 2025 shapes up to be another record-breaking scorcher.

Global climate change is the existential challenge of our lifetimes. Even

1

in the affluent, freeway-centric City of Angels, you can't drive away from firestorms or buy your way out. I'm no scientist—more like a nomadic writer/scholar—but a great many scientists are worried, which worries me. Famed Harvard entomologist and two-time Pulitzer Prize winner Edward O. Wilson long warned about the perils of rapidly declining biodiversity amid a rapidly rising human population. "Our population is too large for safety and comfort," he writes in 2016, with deceptive calm: "Fresh water is growing short, the atmosphere and the seas are increasingly polluted as a result of what has transpired on the land. The climate is changing in ways unfavorable to life, except for microbes, jellyfish, and fungi."[4] The modern genre of disaster films has explored the attack of microbes and an invasion of fungi. Can *Planet of the Jellyfish* be far behind?

I was born in New York City, in wartime 1942, and my return coincided with the global surge of microbes known as COVID-19. Traffic all but vanished. You could stroll down the center of Madison Avenue at midday. Fears of racial violence, spurred by police brutality in far-off Minneapolis, added to the pandemic shutdown as shop owners boarded up display windows in plywood. Climate change isn't to blame for every modern disaster, but its multiple interconnected sources make it the inescapable peril of our time: heat waves, hurricanes, wildfires, and floods, all unprecedented in their terrifying frequency and power. Millions of climate migrants and climate refugees are on the move, as natural disasters come unnaturally thick and fast. People who occupy fortunate interim positions of refuge may well feel a paralyzing sense of doom. A hopeless shrug seems almost reasonable. *What can I do?*

"We tell ourselves stories in order to live," Joan Didion writes.[5] Not just any old story will do, however. Some stories are slow poisons. It can thus help to tell ourselves some occasional real-life and life-affirming success stories. I've never met anyone who didn't like Central Park. Many people say they *love* Central Park. New York City minus Central Park would be unlivable for some. For me too. Maybe we build ourselves parks for the same unstated purpose that we tell ourselves stories, in order to live.

The origin story of Central Park, however life-affirming, can't reverse climate change. Nothing alone, no single action, can unravel or roll back the massive damage or, worse, prevent the looming destruction. Success stories, however, are a resource we cannot afford to neglect, especially when they offer an antidote to depression, hopelessness, and doom-inflected shrugs. I particularly like history-based stories that hit close to home—the actual days of our lives—and I'm happy to have a philosopher on call to endorse my preference for retelling the history-based story of Central Park.

In an assertion that is something of a surprise, at least as coming from a former professor of classical philology who later holds a distinctive version of nihilism, it is the radical, iconoclastic philosopher Friedrich Nietzsche who asserts that the purpose of studying history is to *serve life*.[6]

Why does the story of Central Park, even if life-serving, matter *now*? What makes it urgent? Over half of the world population—56 percent—lives in cities, a figure predicted to rise soon to nearly 70 percent. Asia in 2025 has some thirty megacities with populations over ten million. In Africa, the Nigerian city of Lagos has grown from a population of three hundred thousand in 1950 to an estimated twenty-one million today. People massed in a vast modern metropolis directly impact local and even global environments, and cities are where environmental costs quickly accrue as key contributors to climate change: costs levied in fossil fuels, greenhouse gas emissions, and the byproducts of mass consumption. People are also, however, an invaluable resource in deploying creative low-tech initiatives that directly improve everyday lives. Central Park is literally built by immigrants. Irish and German workers dug the dirt, loaded the horse-drawn carts, blasted the rock, drained the swamps, and planted almost half a million bushes and trees. Today, with refugee tent cities stretching to the horizon and with displaced people yearning for employment, it is far more than an antiquarian inquiry to revisit the mid-nineteenth-century origins of New York City's world-famous Central Park.

A revisitation is not the place for serious policy proposals. Scientific and high-tech projects from underground carbon-capture facilities to remote deserts lined with solar panels all belong to a necessary agenda of present and future interventions. Many visitors, however, don't understand that Central Park is also almost entirely a human invention. A workforce of immigrants often numbering in the thousands created most of the features that we recognize today as the park's apparently "natural" landscape of earth, hills, trees, lakes, meadows, and woods. Even the signature boulders that remain visible reflect human decisions to leave them in place, often for aesthetic reasons, rather than (as happened too) blasted into usable fragments or buried in the topsoil carted by horse from New Jersey.

It is significant for our era of multiple crises to recall that Central Park emerges from a sparsely inhabited wasteland during an especially tumultuous period. Immigrants and refugees flood New York City by the ship-load, so that by 1850 they constitute half the population. It is also a period of intense and bloody national conflict. Slavery divides the country in a simmering crisis throughout the years leading up to the construction of the park. In 1856 a Southern congressman assaults a Northern senator so severely—in the Capitol, no less—that the senator's recovery takes three full years. With the nation tipping toward civil war, Central Park somehow first opens its southernmost features to the public in the winter of 1858 with wild success. Work continues even as the war kills 2 percent of the national population. Dark times do not preclude wise actions. People have walked the paths of Central Park in good times and bad, affirming, if tacitly, that we can reshape our cities to provide oases of beauty and antidotes to hopelessness.

Central Park now receives some forty-two million visitors each year.[7] It outdraws visitors to the city's world-class theaters and museums combined. More than a cost-free tourist destination, Central Park is an everyday fact of life for New Yorkers as well as a perpetual wonder. Imagine a wooded rectangle two miles long and half a mile wide, 843 acres, set deep in the heart of glitzy, sleepless, concrete-and-steel Manhattan. Dog walkers, joggers, birdwatchers, musicians, nannies, bridal parties, children, lovers, and a handful of homeless wanderers make up just a few of its daily visitors. People, many speaking languages I can't identify, seem drawn to the park as if through a dim primal instinct. The crowds prove overwhelmingly peaceful, a mélange of cultures and styles, implicitly respecting the egalitarian values that Frederick Law Olmsted and Calvert Vaux, its designers, understood as fundamental. Despite an origin laced with inequalities and modern episodes of crime and prejudice, Central Park remains an urban refuge. It is also, as a stroll will easily confirm, not just an iconic landmark but preeminently a people's park.

⋮

Every park has a history, but few parks have a story. The origin story of Central Park, beginning immediately before, during, and after the Civil War, shares the turbulent history of New York City, including its chicanery, bigotry, and crime. It is not always a pretty story. The infamous four-day Draft Riot of 1863, for example, specifically targets black workers. White rioters set fire to the Colored Orphan Asylum, and Lincoln ultimately diverts wartime regiments to restore order. Central Park as the first major US public works project offers jobs to the Irish and German immigrants willing to shovel muck and to cart topsoil for a dollar a day. The park also owes its origin, however, to newspaper editors and social elites who lobby for a municipal park befitting the prestige of a city that only in recent years had replaced Philadelphia as the national hub of finance, wealth, and commerce. Central Park both in its origins and in its changes constitutes a story worth telling anytime, perhaps at least once each generation, but it is a story whose successes matter anew today as grounds for hope as we face the unprecedented dilemmas of global climate change.

There is no way to sugarcoat the damages. Black landowners who lost their homes to eminent domain likely did not love Central Park. A few terrible crimes occur, especially during the wilderness years of the 1970s when drugs and muggings prevail. There is also no way to sugarcoat the far vaster global damage. Thousand-year floods now seem annual events. Each year one billion birds smash into US skyscrapers, littering the sidewalks. The hottest ocean temperatures in four hundred years pose an "existential threat" to Australia's Great Barrier Reef.[8] It won't work to blame Mother Nature. We humans have mass-produced the greenhouse gases that now choke the atmosphere, broil the planet, and wreak havoc on the natural world. Unless you live off the grid, grow your own food, and communicate by smoke signal, we are all complicit, as the sea levels inexorably rise. The highest grossing film of all time during the first decade of the twenty-first century was the 1997 bonanza *Titanic*. Disaster seems now all too familiar, as the unsinkable ocean liner goes under. Central Park nonetheless, in its origins, in its shortcomings, and in its changes, offers solid if neglected grounds for hope as we face the dangers of climate change that remain largely of our own making.

Stories traditionally need heroes, even superheroes, and Frederick Law Olmsted has achieved almost heroic stature today as the creator of Central Park and as the father of American landscape design. The accolades are well deserved, but not at the start. Olmsted's later career is impressive, including his design for the grounds of the US Capitol and for Boston's famous 1,100-acre chain of linked parkland known as the Emerald Necklace. In 2015, joining contemporaries such as Emerson, Whitman, and Thoreau, he achieved his own volume in a prominent series featuring classic American writers.[9] His nine-volume papers reappear in 2022 in an online edition, and a dedicated website (Olmsted.org) even helps celebrate his two hundredth birthday. When he first begins work at Central Park, however, he is a failed surveyor, failed clerk, lapsed farmer, out-of-work editor, and an impoverished journalist in his mid-thirties. Indeed, Olmsted is a mostly directionless young man with no experience in landscape design, until he lands a modest job working for the park's chief engineer. Central Park offers an oblique criticism, too, of our need for heroes or for the addictive great-man theories of history. His lesser-known partner at Central Park, Calvert Vaux, twice comes to Olmsted's rescue.

A deemphasis on heroes opens up space to focus on more human-scale, collective, and collaborative actions. The creation of Central Park takes more than a village. It takes almost a decade of heated discussion in elite parlors and in gritty newspaper editorials. Receiving initial state funding in 1853, Central Park marks its official completion in 1876, after more than twenty years of financial crises, social conflict, and open civil war. London-born Vaux, as a recently naturalized US citizen, is especially sensitive to the democratic ideals of equality that he sees embodied in Central Park. Our nineteenth-century ancestors left us, in effect, a vast, artificial, living monument built from trees, water, soil, rocks, meadows, and woodlands. It offers evidence of what the imagination can achieve in transforming urban landscapes, improving everyday lives, and making vital, measurable contributions to urban environments. Climate change can't be altered overnight, but reflecting on the origins of Central Park may well empower people to address the crisis in their own towns and cities—perhaps one big park at a time.

▮▮▮

A parable is not a history. Two brilliant histories, *Before Central Park* (2022) by Sara Cedar Miller and *The Park and the People* (1992) by Roy Rosenzweig and Elizabeth Blackmar, constitute an indispensable treasury of historical research that I've relied on throughout. Parables indeed are less like histories than like rainbows, and in fact rainbows are the classic example of a parabolic arc. As the curved distance between two points, parabolic arcs and rainbows follow an algebraic equation ($y = ax^2 + bx + c$) that clearly does not apply to parables as a minor literary genre. While fables tend to exhaust their meaning in a lesson that even a tortoise and a hare can convey, parables in their arc and span tend to embrace a mysterious excess that resists full explanation, unlike Aesop's rabbits and turtles. Kafka writes that parables traffic in "the ungraspable."[10] Central Park too embraces an excessive, ungraspable appeal, accessible even to visitors simply strolling through the woods, pausing for photographs along the bridges, or renting a boat to row around the artificial lake. "Every inducement should be offered visitors to ramble and wander about," as Olmstead advises concerning another park-making project.[11] Central Park in its parabolic curvature extending from past to present creates an ideal space for reflective wandering.

Most people see pretty clearly the global changes taking place, despite climate deniers. The big question is not whether climate change is real, or even (as a fact of life) whether humans created it, but rather what are we going to do about it?

1

¦¦¦

Once Upon a Time in 1857

IT IS EARLY AUGUST 1857, and Frederick Olmsted is down on his luck. At thirty-five, after a series of false starts in choosing a career, offset by a few modest successes as a travel writer, he is secluded in a Connecticut seaside inn writing a series for the *New-York Daily Tribune* entitled "The Southerners at Home." The small payment he receives will not pay off his debts. He can't afford coal when the temperature drops, and the innkeeper will soon demand room payment, which he can't afford either. Luckily, this afternoon he will be meeting a prominent family friend for tea. Charles Elliott is a man of diverse interests, now a businessman in ironworks and vice president of the infant New York City Republican Party, who has previously spent eight years as a landscape gardener. Olmsted does not know that Elliott is also on the eleven-man Board of Commissioners newly appointed by the state legislature to oversee the construction of Central Park.

Frederick puts down his steel-point pen, which has replaced the quill as an emblem of modern progress. The plate-glass Crystal Palace in London recently hosted the Great Exhibition of 1851 showcasing steam-driven machines. Tea and hometown conversation at least promise a distraction from the solitude of writing and a grumbling stomach. Perhaps Frederick wonders what twist of fate has brought him to this strange seaside financial impasse. A sometime New Yorker, he has heard talk about the large new park planned for uptown Manhattan—it has been in the news—but it may be close to the last thing on his mind today. He has apparently found his calling as a traveling journalist, after episodes as a seaman and two tries as a farmer, but his prospects have dried up and his money has run out.

The nation, while Frederick is running low on prospects and cash, is running out of time. In the fall of 1855, just two years earlier, he had been busy collecting donations to buy rifles for antislavery settlers in the Kansas territory.

Bleeding Kansas is the epithet that Horace Greeley, founding editor of the *New-York Daily Tribune*, applies to the bloody, violence-gripped territory facing the decision whether to enter the Union as a slave state or free. Proslavery mobs slip across the border from Missouri on guerilla raids, targeting free-state settlers. John Brown, pursuing his self-proclaimed mission from God to eradicate slavery, arrives in Kansas with antislavery reinforcements, swords in hand, and they hack some unlucky proslavers limb from limb. Learning that the antislavery settlers are well supplied with rifles, Frederick changes plan and ships them a twelve-pound brass mountain howitzer with its mounting carriage.[1] "I always proclaim myself a *dangerous man*," he writes in a letter at twenty-six. "I know that I am. I know that there is danger in my opinions—danger to the *basis of society* and all that."[2]

Bronze smoothbore M1841 12-pounder howitzer at Gettysburg National Battlefield. Djmaschek, CC BY-SA 4.0, via Wikimedia Commons.

Olmsted's views on slavery suggest someone finding his way, engaged but independent. Connecticut friends push him to adopt their abolitionist views, but he initially supports the Free-Soil party, active between 1848 and 1854. Free-Soilers, as they are called, oppose slavery, but they specifically oppose the extension of slavery into the Western territories. Although Frederick believes that slavery is immoral, he is not ready to embrace abolition with its unknown consequences for enslaved blacks. He also doesn't know exactly what constitutional remedy is best for the nation, since slavery is legal in Southern states. Neither does Abraham Lincoln, who also believes that slaveholding is immoral. At his inauguration in 1861, he is actively seeking compromises with the South to hold the Union together. A mountain howitzer skirts constitutional questions while giving the antislavery settlers in Kansas a means of self-defense. It does not solve or even address a race-based slave system that nothing short of civil war will, very imperfectly, resolve.

New York City, where I was born just months after America entered World War II, is still a scene of conflicts that date back to Olmsted's day, but the conflicts now extend beyond racism. Greenhouse gases threaten not just the nation but the entire planet. It is hard to focus on the rising global temperature, however, as my plane banks toward LaGuardia. Suddenly I glimpse a vast rectangle of green. Central Park! After a moment of wonder, my thoughts—I can't help it—shift to the puzzle of all that real estate lying there vacant. Soon I can make out grassy fields, baseball diamonds, and two large, irregular, silver-gray sheets of water reflecting the cloud cover. More than fifty miles of walking paths crisscross the park, disappearing beneath the summertime green canopy. One question keeps returning. How did this miracle ever occur?

The construction of Central Park, from its initial funding in 1853 to its official completion in 1876, parallels the rebuilding of America. Its creation requires not only legal acts of property seizure that displace mainly impoverished minorities but also battlefield-worthy supplies of gunpower employed to blast through rock and re-engineer nature. It also coincides with the emergence of New York City as the nation's preeminent metropolis, for which Central Park quickly becomes a symbol. Enjoyed at first mainly by upper-crust New Yorkers who live nearby or can afford carriages, a little later it also provides a weekend haven for poor immigrants flooding into the city and packed into tenements. Unlike the Statue of Liberty which arrives in 1885, it is both rooted in the landscape and intrinsic to an experience of the city. Tourists still seek out the nostalgic horse-drawn carriage rides that begin in 1863, then at a cost of twenty-five cents, now well over a hundred dollars per hour. Central Park, however, is more than a New York City icon. It is a success story with global significance as we struggle to find collective and effective responses to the worldwide dangers of climate change.

Plane rides offer a bird's-eye view, much like the so-called supertall apartment buildings—ultrathin pencil box towers—that offer panoramic upper-floor views. Magazine articles and real estate ads similarly depict a spacious emerald rectangle spread out amid the surrounding city like a magic carpet. At ground level the view is less awe-inspiring amid crowds, cabs, e-bikes, delivery trucks, and sidewalks hooded with scaffolding. Central Park may be an advertiser's dream and a taxi driver's obstacle, but it is also a visionary gift from the past. It belongs not only to the ultrarich who can afford a spectacular view. It belongs as well to the people—nameless and forgotten—who did the actual construction and to the people who arrive every day carrying their picnic baskets and roller skates.

Such thoughts are what drive me at eighty, when I'd rather be sleeping late, to mull over the question of how Central Park came about. The story clearly requires the crucial presence of Frederick Olmsted, but it is more than a one-man show. The invention of Central Park, beyond myths of heroic individualism, depends upon shared desires, unlikely partnerships, civic vision, long-range planning, creative improvisation, and, yes, some blind luck. Our nineteenth-century ancestors, embroiled in a war over slavery, certainly got something right. Central Park in my view is what makes New York City *livable*. Diehards of course will roll their eyes, but New York City *minus* Central Park? Please count me out.

Central Park, beyond whether you love or hate New York City, deserves respect as the achievement of people living in dangerous times. The newest military munition in the late 1840s—the hollow-based Minié ball—is expressly designed to shatter bones. Soldiers can survive a flesh wound, but shattered bone is almost guaranteed to kill from toxic infections. It is during the prewar years, when Frederick ships a mountain howitzer to Kansas, that New Yorkers are also hotly debating the creation of a large public park. Central Park is the first major urban public park in America and the model for a new concept of public property held in trust for cultural purposes.[3] It is also an expression of American democracy at a moment when the nation and its principles are under immense stress. Central Park represents, in its underlying values, the promise of American democracy. Olmsted, of course, thinks none of these thoughts as he waits to meet Charles Elliott over tea in Connecticut at Morris Cove.

Central Park in the era of climate change holds special importance as a success story with global implications. It also bears the distinctive marks of its nineteenth-century origins, which also bear significance today. While Olmsted is sometimes (wrongly) credited as the lone creator of Central Park, it is the state-appointed Board of Commissioners, political appointees all, that *chooses* the Greensward plan over its competitors. The Republican state legislature appoints six Republican commissioners to the eleven-person board, so that local politics certainly plays a role in its choice. Moreover, Olmsted and his underappreciated partner Calvert Vaux have barely met, neither qualified to design a park, and their partnership depends on a daisy chain of wild improbabilities. Gaia today needs all the resources we can muster—amateur and professional, likely and unlikely, even luck and parables—as we seek to address the unprecedented crisis of our lifetimes.

My own improbable path brings me back to New York City after years spent wandering and following my heart. After my wife of thirty years died from a long illness, my heart and a dating app eventually led me to Margot—talented, funny, with a radiant smile—my partner now for the last six years. The big surprise: she lives in an apartment directly across from Central Park. I drink my morning coffee looking into the green mid-canopy and later take four-mile walks in the park without meeting a stoplight. What I don't see on my walks is also significant. The frisky park squirrels can make me forget that wildlife populations have plunged on average 69 percent since 1970.[4] The occasional city rat scuttling along a drainage ditch is a survivor. Central Park, as an enduring gift from ancestors living almost two centuries ago, offers more than a vast green space amid a surrounding field of concrete. It can provide a resource to think with and to think about as we navigate into a threatening and highly uncertain future.

∎∎∎

Frederick Law Olmsted is the indispensable figure when we think about the origins of Central Park. His significance grows exponentially, however, after Central Park, when he adds many more parks to his résumé—seventeen in which he or his associates play a major role. He also plays a supporting

Frederick Law Olmsted (c. 1895). Bartlett F. Henney, from a photo by James Notman, courtesy of the National Park Service.

role in creating the beloved system of national parks. (It is his son, Frederick Olmsted Jr., who in 1916 helps write the enabling federal legislation.) He even ages into the iconic visual likeness of a bearded patriarch. The caption accompanying an engraved magazine illustration appearing in the 1890s describes him as "The Most Distinguished American Landscape Architect." His eyes, however, if you look closely, might suggest beneath the patriarchal image a skeptical Victorian sage who at any moment just might, like Darwin or Lyell, put everything in doubt or send a howitzer to Kansas—a man with opinions dangerous to the *basis of society* and all that. Fearless, confident, and not quite steady of mind, he leads a park-centered movement in landscape design that alters more than the shape of the land.

There are several problems with a hasty canonization of Frederick Law Olmsted. First, he is thirty-five, broke, and unemployed when in 1857 he luckily manages to land a temporary job as park superintendent for an un-built urban park, and his duties amount to little more than overseeing the crews already clearing the site. Second, his later role as architect-in-chief is inconceivable without the help of Calvert Vaux. Vaux, whose surname rhymes with *rocks*, is a young British architect recently arrived in New York, and it is Vaux who recruits Olmsted to work on the winning design for Central Park. Without Vaux, Olmsted might be remembered mostly as a talented, minor mid-century journalist and travel writer.

"I brought as much as you to the park," Vaux later reminds Olmsted, somewhat testily, and he is right.[5] Vaux rarely receives due credit, even though he creates most of the park's indispensable architectural features. Although Vaux is an equal partner in creating the Greensward plan, it is Olmsted who is awarded the salaried position of architect-in-chief, despite his zero credentials in architecture. Vaux meanwhile is hired as an assis-tant, paid by the hour, and only in 1859 does he receive the delayed title of "consulting architect."[6] Olmsted acquiesces in the unequal arrangement, although in no position to protest, and only later, in 1865, do they establish a true partnership when they create the landscape firm Olmsted, Vaux & Company. The partnership holds until 1872, when they amicably dissolve the firm and Olmsted relocates to Boston. Vaux remains in New York, de-fending Central Park against proposals that would mutilate their crowning achievement.

A final problem with the canonization of Olmsted is that Central Park remains under construction until 1876, long after Olmsted has left. One benefit in modestly decanonizing Olmsted, despite his acknowledged im-portance, lies in recognizing that Central Park embodies in its very struc-ture a principle of change. The landscape is in continuous motion, includ-ing periods of decline and renewal. No one thus can experience Central Park as a single, steady object of vision, no matter how high up you live in a supertall. We encounter it only piecemeal, in glimpses or visits, which vary with the terrain and the weather. Morning dog walkers experience the park differently than do loving couples secluded among its shrubs or boulders. Central Park is almost the opposite of a changeless monolith. Its appearance alters not only by the hour as the light alters, like the grain-stacks painted by Monet, but also year by year. Visitors often develop a personal route or favorite bench. The principle of change implies, as seems to happen without effort, that we all possess our own distinctive and ever-changing Central Parks.

What doesn't change in Central Park is its power as a visionary proto-type. The massive greenspace within the heart of New York City is a model for urban projects, but it is also a tribute to multigenerational commit-ments. Although it takes its political origin in a vision of "the people," it is also the product of social dialogue that transcends politics. Multiple voices participate in the discussions that lead to its creation, including vocal oppo-nents such as the downtown merchants who resent taxpayer funds used to benefit uptown property owners and, worse, land speculators. The polyglot voices engaged in the creation of the park embody a process that, however messy, is nonetheless at heart profoundly democratic. "I give the sign of democracy," writes Walt Whitman in *Leaves of Grass* (1855). "By God! I will accept nothing which all cannot have their counterpart of on the same terms."[7] He self-publishes his call amid the debate that culminates in Central Park.

Central Park as a prototype also offers a model for thinking big. Big thinking is not common, despite moon shots and theme parks, and it is es-pecially valuable in times of crisis. Skeptics, pragmatists, penny-pinchers, and defenders of the status quo keep advising us to play it safe and hedge our bets. The pressing question for the age of climate change may be less how *did* Central Park happen, which is an historical issue, than how *could* it happen? How, we might ask similarly, can we create a legacy for future generations that makes a visionary contribution to the ongoing quality of life? Big thinking, I suspect, is the answer.

Andrew Jackson Downing is the big-thinking young wunderkind editor of a popular journal called *The Horticulturist*, and he proves immensely important both indirectly in the creation of Central Park and directly in the lives of Olmsted and Vaux. "Nobody, whether he be rich or poor, builds a house or lays out a garden without consulting Downing's works," claims novelist Catharine Maria Sedgwick (1789–1867). "Every young couple who sets up housekeeping buys them."[8] Olmsted, even after his rise to the status of patriarch, describes Downing as "the greatest master in America of landscape-gardening."[9] At twenty-six Downing publishes *A Treatise on the Theory and Practice of Landscape Gardening* (1841), which instantly establishes him as an authority on gardens, landscapes, and all matters horticultural. He follows up the next year with *Cottage Residences* (1842),

Andrew Jackson Downing (1851). Frontispiece to an 1875 edition of *A Treatise on the Theory and Practice of Landscape Gardening* (Boston: C. C. Little & Co., 1841).

and, as the capstone of an astonishing decade, he later publishes *The Architecture of Country Houses* (1850). His most influential role in shaping public opinion, however, doubtless comes with his work as founding editor of *The Horticulturist and Journal of Rural Art and Rural Taste*, which begins publication in 1846. Its publisher describes it as, after the Bible, the most widely read publication in America.[10] *The Horticulturist* also advocates strongly for a New York City park.

Downing's landscape firm in Newburgh, sixty miles north of Manhattan and overlooking the Hudson River, includes a nursery, and Olmsted in his farming years once journeys there to buy fruit trees. As Downing's

fame spreads, he accepts commissions that increasingly require architectural features, which is how he comes to hire a young London architect,
Calvert Vaux. Vaux soon rises to the position of full partner, collaborating
on Downing's commissions and learning the fundamentals of landscape
design. Downing's most significant commission comes from President
Fillmore, who in 1851 approves his appointment to lay out the grounds
between the Capitol and the White House.[11] That same year Downing
publishes a long editorial in *The Horticulturist*: "The leading topic of town
gossip and newspaper paragraphs just now, in New-York," the editorial
begins, "is the new park proposed by Mayor Kingsland." The town gossip includes a number of alternative sites for a new park, and Downing
makes no secret of his scorn for the current urban landscape. "What are
called parks in New-York," he scoffs, "are not even apologies for the thing;
they are only squares, or paddocks."[12] It is time to think big, and Downing
would be everyone's choice to design the new Central Park.

Downing is returning home to Newburgh in July 1852 on the steamboat
Henry Clay, packed with five hundred passengers as it makes its sched-
uled Hudson River run from Albany to Manhattan. A boiler explodes. Fire
sweeps through the ship, passengers leap overboard, and fifty people die
in the worst steamboat disaster ever on the Hudson River. Downing is
an expert swimmer, but he drowns trying to save his fellow passengers.
The Horticulturist soon publishes a memorial illustration showing the hillside view from his Newburgh estate, with a sailboat on the calm river and
mountains in the background: a perfect nineteenth-century picturesque
landscape. The accompanying article laments a loss that extends to the
entire nation, "so shocking and so sudden."

2

Olmsted Seeking Olmsted

FREDERICK LAW OLMSTED is a slow, uncertain, start-and-stop work in progress. He shows that you don't need to know what you want to be. You can experiment, try new things, keep changing, and, if you're lucky, just slip into the right niche, not so much finding a career as wandering around until your career finds you. How does Frederick Law Olmsted become the acknowledged patriarch of American landscape design? Almost by accident.

Accident is not the right term if it implies random luck, good or bad, as when a lottery winner defies the odds.[1] Something besides higher math is at play as Olmsted takes his first unsteady steps into adulthood. His mother has died young, and his father sends him away for schooling to live with "country parsons of small poor parishes," as Frederick later puts it. "I was strangely uneducated—miseducated," he continues.[2] His father soon gives him a job in the family dry-goods business, selling fine silks and other such expensive retail items, but Frederick chooses to apprentice with a surveyor. After a two-year apprenticeship, however, he says farewell to a surveyor's life and returns to live with his wealthy father in Hartford, the inland state capital of Connecticut. He doesn't stay long. His father again arranges an apprenticeship for his restless son with a dry-goods supplier in New York City.

Frederick, already showing signs of his lifelong vagabond tendencies, in 1840 moves to Brooklyn, then quite rural, and commutes by ferry to the dry-goods firm in Manhattan. He quickly tires again of the garment business. The next step is obvious for an impressionable young man who has read the just-published memoir *Two Years Before the Mast* (1840). He goes to sea. He signs on with a China-bound merchant vessel as a "ship's boy," lowest of a lowly lot, paid four to eight dollars per month. Perpetually seasick, he rarely leaves the ship during the rugged ten-month voyage under a captain so harsh that, on the return, a crew member successfully sues him for abuse. Frederick has no further interest in a nautical life.

Once back on land, he is still figuratively at sea. He lacks the academic credentials for admission to nearby Yale, unlike his older brother John, a future physician. His irregular schooling, the product of a childhood eye ailment and a tendency to daydream, has hardly prepared him for rigorous study.[3] A firm self-confidence, however, never seems to desert him, and Frederick at times even teeters on the brink of arrogance, as a photograph from his late twenties may suggest. Although unqualified for admission, he follows John to Yale and gets listed as a "special student," although he mostly just hangs out with John's circle of friends. A born romantic, he is smitten with Elizabeth Baldwin, whose father is governor of Connecticut. Elizabeth introduces him to the work of contemporary poets, philosophers, and theologians, which initiates a major change in his self-regard and future self-education. She also, however, breaks his heart. His stint as a special student thus lasts just three months, and its main benefit—perhaps not entirely appreciated—is a new sense of his intellectual powers. He afterward always keeps the books of important writers at his bedside, including the essays of Ralph Waldo Emerson, just twenty years older and a now-famous New Englander.

Frederick is hardly alone in his attraction to Emerson's kinetic prose— swooping from philosophical abstractions to corn and melons and up into the realm of spirit. "I was simmering, simmering, simmering," as Walt Whitman famously remarked. "Emerson brought me to a boil."[4] Frederick does not exactly boil over. He rather quickly informs his father about an entirely new desire. He decides to be a farmer.

███

The choice of farming is not random, as farming then holds a mystique beyond its ancient connections with the land. Watt's steam engine, Whitney's

Frederick Law Olmsted (1850). Frontispiece, *Frederick Law Olmsted: Landscape Architect, 1822–1903*, ed. Frederick Law Olmsted Jr. and Theodora Kimball (New York: G. P. Putnam's Sons, 1922).

cotton gin, and McCormick's reaper reflect a mechanical spirt of invention that carries over to agriculture. Everyone, it seems, is an amateur horticulturalist. Gentleman farmers, as distinct from subsistence farmers, possess the leisure and means to study the latest scientific literature on agriculture. Frederick of course subscribes to *The Horticulturist*.

There is something new and distinctively American in what may look or feel like wandering or even floundering. Emerson's famous essay "Self-Reliance" (1841) urges Americans to turn away from sophisticated European exemplars. "A sturdy lad from New Hampshire or Vermont, who in turn tries all the professions," Emerson begins, "who *teams it, farms it, peddles*, keeps a school, preaches, edits a newspaper, goes to Congress, buys a township, and so forth, in successive years, and always, like a cat, falls on his feet, is worth a hundred of these city dolls." Frederick, no city doll, at least has a gritty knack for landing on his feet. "He walks abreast with his days," Emerson concludes of the catlike, self-reliant soul, "and feels no shame in not 'studying a profession,' for he does not postpone his life, but lives already."[5] Frederick, a sturdy New England lad, walks abreast with his days right smack into a sixty-acre potato farm on the Connecticut coast, which his father agreeably buys for him.

Frederick's first trial as a gentleman farmer fails conclusively. No loafer, he has prepared by working for a season as a farmhand with a noted agricultural reformer. The potato farm, however, is run down, the soil rocky, and the crop dismal. No worries. Olmsted *père* buys his catlike son a much better, larger farm, at three times the cost. Frederick names it Tosomock Farm, likely in tribute to its original Dutch owner, named Teaschenmaker.[6] The 130 fertile acres on Staten Island offer improved financial prospects, as well as a picturesque location overlooking Raritan Bay. It is 1848, Frederick is twenty-six, and it looks as if he has finally found his niche—for the moment.

Frederick, whose self-reliance owes a strong debt to his generous father, proves nowhere more Emersonian than in his commitment to *melioration*: Emerson's term for persistent improvements, moral as well as material. Olmsted's lifelong commitment to melioration takes a typical material form at Tosomock Farm when, for example, he transforms a puddled depression used for washing wagons into an ornamental pond ringed with stones. It is not hard to imagine the same spirit at work in Central Park, where Olmsted and Vaux are concerned with melioration, moral as well as material. Central Park, Olmsted writes, "exercises a distinctly harmonizing and refining influence upon the most unfortunate and most lawless classes of the city—an influence favorable to courtesy, self-control, and temperance."[7]

Melioration for Olmsted, no matter how extended its moral reach, always seems to begin with practical, material improvements. He subscribes to multiple farming journals and studies new techniques for drainage. He decides that Tosomock Farm, formerly planted in wheat, will provide a better return if he raises fruits and vegetables, since the new railroads put local wheat farmers in direct competition with long-distance growers. Perishable goods like fruits and vegetables fare far better in local markets. He also orders five thousand fruit tree saplings—it's easy to imagine who pays the bill—which he plants, as he later writes, "with my own hands."

In 1852 his pears win a local prize. Downing even publishes Frederick's article about pears in *The Horticulturist*. Clearly taking the famed editor as his model, Frederick joins two local organizations for advancing the "rural arts." He can't know that the improvements he makes to his Staten Island farm foreshadow the massive improvements that will lie ahead in Central Park.

Tosomock Farm also demonstrates Frederick's genius for organization. He manages six hired hands on an hourly schedule, requiring his foreman to report daily before supper.[8] Something has changed in his mentality. He adds multiple specimen trees—black walnut, mulberry, linden, elms, ginkgo, and even two cedars of Lebanon—while converting a carriage path into a dramatic curved driveway, draining marshes to add tillable acreage, and moving outbuildings to improve the view from his two-story farmhouse. He diversifies his crops with corn, cabbage, lima beans, and raspberries. He is too busy to indulge his habit of daydreaming, but it would be a mistake to conclude that he is fully committed to a straightforward path as farmer. His path keeps taking unforeseen twists and turns.

It is axiomatic that the farmer takes a wife. Frederick, as his brother John writes, "would marry almost anybody that would let him."[9] John in 1851 soon marries a Tosomock neighbor, Mary Perkins, despite his serious lung hemorrhage. Frederick has been courting—or flirting with—a former Hartford neighbor, and he soon summons up a marriage proposal. The young woman promptly accepts. Then, just as abruptly, she breaks off the engagement. Is she dismayed at learning that her pragmatic future husband plans to delay their marriage until he can bring sixty thousand cabbages to market? Frederick seems happy enough after the breakup that his father wonders if he "brought it about purposely."[10] The idyll of Tosomock Farm does not last long either. Frederick decides to go on his travels.

***

John has planned a three-month walking tour in Europe, and Frederick can't resist. He dutifully asks his father for permission to leave after spring planting, as his father holds the mortgage on Tosomock Farm. His father as usual agrees, even funding the trip. After hiring a farmhand to care for the fruit trees, in late spring 1850 Frederick departs with John on a steamship bound for Liverpool.

The Opening of Birkenhead Park (1847). *The Illustrated London News,* April 10, 1847.

"The soul is no traveller," Emerson advises; "the wise man stays at home." "Travelling," he adds, "is a fool's paradise."[11] Emerson eventually softens his attitude toward travel, admitting its well-known opportunities for learning. Opportunity strikes swiftly! A Liverpool baker happens to mention that the Olmsted brothers should visit the recently opened 220-acre Birkenhead Park. A woodcut depicts crowds and carriages gathered at the opening of the "People's Park," as it is called, England's first publicly funded municipal park. Frederick is dazzled. The Grand Entrance, a six-story edifice with a triple-arched arcade fronted by twelve Ionic columns, quickly funnels visitors into a rural landscape of serpentine rolled-gravel paths, shrubs and flowers, lodges, temples, bridges, and even a music pavilion. "Five minutes of admiration," Frederick writes later, "and a few more spent in studying the manner in which art had been employed to obtain from nature so much beauty, and I was ready to admit that in democratic America there was nothing to be thought of as comparable with this People's Garden. Indeed, gardening had here reached a perfection that I had never before dreamed of."[12]

"Wonderful intricacy in the web," writes Emerson in *The Conduct of Life* (1860), "wonderful constancy in the design this vagabond life admits."[13] Frederick on his zigzag path toward an unknown goal returns to Tosomock Farm in October, just in time for the fall harvest. The web is already shifting. The Staten Island gentleman farmer—apprentice surveyor, dry-goods clerk, ship's boy, and Yale special student—experiences another twist in the road. "Shoulder your duds," Walt Whitman urges, "and I will mine, and let us hasten forth. Wonderful cities and free nations we shall fetch as we go."[14] Frederick, heeding the wayfarer's vagabond call of the open road, leaves New York to become a travel writer.

3

###

Paperback Writer

FREDERICK'S YOUNG STATEN ISLAND neighbor George Putnam has just come up with a terrific new idea: the paperback book.[1] The name Putnam soon becomes well known in the publishing industry, beginning with George's insight that a newly literate public will want low-cost books. Paperbacks cut the cost to mass-market budgets, although Putnam misses the stampede toward dime novels. Beadle and Adams does not, with the New York publishing firm cranking out some seven thousand Wild West "blood and thunder" titles by the end of the century.[2] Putnam's most immediate dilemma, however, is a lack of content. Might neighbor Olmsted happen to have a manuscript describing his recent tour abroad?

Frederick in short order hands Putnam a seven-hundred-page manuscript. Putnam shrewdly splits the text into two volumes, published as *Walks and Talks of an American Farmer in England*. Volume 1, appearing in 1852, omits Frederick's name from the title page, but he is suddenly at thirty a published author, albeit anonymous. Even his prizewinning pears won't keep him down on the farm. In addition, a select circle knows about his authorship, including Andrew Downing. Downing cuts a dashing figure with his brooding eyes and flowing black hair. A Swedish-born writer describes Downing as "what people call here *a self-made man*, that is to say, a man who has less to thank education for what he is than his own endeavors."[3] Frederick, a self-made man still in the making, has remade himself once again.

▐▐▐

Frederick Olmsted's delayed and winding road to Central Park might prove a useful metaphor as we navigate the perils ahead. Hope includes a steady trust in what is ultimately unknowable: "an alternative," as Rebecca Solnit writes, "to the certainty of both optimists and pessimists."[4] When Frederick returns from his travels abroad in October 1850, he does not foresee a career in travel writing, and it will be seven years until he hits bottom, or an apparent dead end, at Morris Cove Inn, where broke and futureless he learns about a job supervising cleanup crews. Before his work at Central Park is finished, however, he will have published three travel books. The subtitle of his best-known work, *The Cotton Kingdom* (1861), begins with the phrase *A Traveller's Observations*.[5] Olmsted does not invoke travel as an Emersonian metaphor for life as a web of unanticipated connections. It is a literal term describing his journeys in the American South, but it also applies to his twisting vagabond life on the road, which will soon take another major turn.

"Sit a while wayfarer," advises Whitman in *Leaves of Grass* (1855): "Long enough have you dreamed contemptible dreams,/Now I wash the gum from your eyes./You must habit yourself to the dazzle of the light and of every moment of your life."[6] Frederick, in a hurry, is not inclined to sit a while, nor, like Walt, to loaf and invite his soul. *The Horticulturist* in 1853 publishes a very positive review of *Walks and Talks*. Unsigned, the review of volume one is likely written by Downing, who in *The Horticulturist* two years earlier had published a long anonymous descriptive passage entitled "The People's Park at Birkenhead, Near Liverpool." The passage later appears verbatim in *Walks and Talks*.[7] Significantly, in suggesting how he sees himself, Frederick signs his anonymous passage in *The Horticulturist* with the pen name Wayfarer.

Wayfarer is a pen name not chosen lightly. Whitman in *Leaves of Grass* makes the open road both a personal signature and a metaphor for the national spirit. "Afoot and light-hearted, I take to the open road,/Healthy, free, the world before me,/The long brown path before me, leading wherever I choose."[8] Whitman's allusion to the final lines of *Paradise Lost*— "The world was all before them, where to choose"—suggests a New Adam in the New World. Another traveler in America celebrated Whitman's open road for creating a deep, powerful, and original myth. "It is a new great doctrine. A doctrine of life," writes D. H. Lawrence. "The great home of the Soul is the open road. Not heaven, not paradise. Not *above*. Not even *within.* The soul is neither *above* nor *within.* It is a wayfarer down the open road."[9] An era of border closings and climate-change migrations will test how far the open road retains its almost mythic power. For Frederick, the open road is not a great new doctrine but the winding path that leads him to Central Park. Central Park is not a destination, and even as a stopover it has far less to do with Lawrence's soul than with Whitman's politics.

■■■

Olmsted is already well aware that the idea of a public park contains political implications. His anonymous passage on Birkenhead Park in *The Horticulturist,* for example, includes his lament that "democratic America" has nothing yet to compare with Liverpool's People's Park.[10] "It is republican in its very idea and tendency," Downing writes about the prospect of a large public park in New York City.[11] He points out, perhaps thanks to Frederick, that Birkenhead Park "has been formed by the people themselves, and not made and presented to them by the sovereign." The people, as a political concept, implies a distinctive American inclusiveness, and Downing's account acknowledges a specific local dilemma of inclusion: "New York, for instance, now one of the largest cities in the world, has no public park whatever, no breathing place, no grounds for the exercise and refreshment of her jaded citizens." *Jaded* here does not mean *bored* or *cloyed.* A jade is a horse broken down from overwork. In a people's republic, Downing implies, New York's overworked citizens, especially its immigrants crowded and cramped into dark, disease-ridden tenements, have an urgent need and political right to a public park.

Newspapers are where the debate over a public park in New York City approaches critical mass. As early as 1844 the editor of the *Evening Post,* poet William Cullen Bryant, recommends a picturesque 154-acre tract along the East River known as Jones Wood.[12] Downing proposes a site centered on Thirty-Ninth Street.[13] Other options are in play, while more mundane controversies over funding continue. Should funds depend on general taxes? Special assessments? A combination? Even the weather adds urgency to the decisions. "The heats of summer are upon us": so Bryant begins his July proposal for a park that promises "shade and recreation." Ambrose Kingsland, the newly elected mayor of New York City, in 1851 creates a special committee charged with comparing potential sites, and in the first official use of the name the committee reports that "the proposition of Central Park is greatly to be preferred."[14] The report changes nothing. Rival bills passed by the Republican-controlled state legislature spark lawsuits and keep the ultimate choice of location suspended in a political-legislative-legal limbo.

Then a break. Once the Jones Wood site dies in court, the city moves quickly to invoke eminent domain and to acquire an initial 778 acres. The Commissioners of Estimate and Assessment—five "eminent gentlemen," as the *Tribune* describes them—begin a two-year process to identify land-owners and authorize payments. Some 1,600 people live in the area designated for the park, many poor, some displaced. A cholera epidemic in 1849 forces pig owners to move their animals uptown, and the removal of "piggeries" from the designated parkland falls hardest on poor Irish immigrants living in what an 1855 woodcut calls a "squatter settlement." Since the owners of 410 lots are unknown, it's not surprising that people take up residence rent-free in abandoned lots. The city owns some of the remaining 7,110 lots, but the eminent gentlemen face a herculean task. Removals range from German immigrants raising vegetables in well-kept gardens to bone-boiling businesses producing charcoal to make sugar. The lingering stench from swamps and piggeries is perhaps hardest to remove.

SQUATTER SETTLEMENT, 1855.—NOW CENTRAL PARK.

Squatter Settlement, 1855—Now Central Park (c. 1870–1879). New York Public Library Digital Collections.

Seneca Village, located on the Upper West Side, offers a stark contrast to the ramshackle properties located elsewhere in the designated parkland. The residents of Seneca Village live in a settled community, where two-thirds are African American and almost half of them own their homes, an extremely high percentage given the civil, legal, and social obstacles to black ownership of land. Seneca Village is also a mixed community. Sarah Wilson, an African American woman who washes laundry for a living, acquires her property in Seneca Village through the help of white neighbors named Wagstaff. Philip Dunn, a middle-aged Irish policeman, lives in a house owned by Willa Pease, an African American grocer. "Most of the village residents," historian Sara Cedar Miller writes, "worked as unskilled manual laborers, porters, sailors, gardeners, service-industry workers, and domestics."[15] No matter. Seneca Village and its residents are swept away.

Although Seneca Village occupies a relatively high bluff, known as Summit Rock, where the land is sloped but flat, Central Park reclaims mostly rough, irregular terrain that an official document describes as "abrupt and rocky elevations, intersected constantly by ravines and gentle valleys." The site is largely an uninviting wasteland of boulders, gullies, and fetid bogs, "entirely useless for building purposes."[16] The park, created in this unbuildable urban quasi-wasteland, increases to its current 843 acres in 1859 when the uptown boundary is extended four blocks north. The true *annus mirabilis*, however, is 1853, when the state legislature actually allocates funds to purchase the land for an unnamed park in New York City.

Frederick meanwhile is focused on travel writing. The second volume of *Walks and Talks*, dedicated to "the memory of A. J. Downing," has the misfortune to appear in the same year as *Uncle Tom's Cabin* (1852). Harriet Beecher Stowe's sentimental antislavery novel breaks all records as it sells an unheard-of ten thousand copies in its first week. Her abolitionist sympathies underlie episodes designed to draw tears, enlisting emotion and the heart's truth in the service of reform, although her attendant religious vision of black suffering as redemptive mars the book for many readers today. The *New-York Daily Times*—later the *New York Times*—decides in response to run nonfiction reports to oppose what even Frederick (a distant relative of Stowe) calls "spoony fancy pictures" of Southern life.[17] Stowe, after all, never sets foot outside New England, and the South remains for most Northern readers largely terra incognita. The *Times* is looking for a writer who will send back firsthand and fact-based reports.

A young farmer on Staten Island, as it happens, has just published a book about his walks and talks in England. A friend arranges the meeting. Seizing another opportunity, Frederick on December 11, 1852, abandons

Tosomock Farm and takes to the road as a traveling correspondent for the *New-York Daily Times*.

■■■

Central Park in 1852 is not even a solid idea when Frederick, age thirty, begins his travels in the Deep South. He makes his way by foot, mule, train, and steamboat, and his New England accent will expose him as a stranger—worse, a Yankee—as soon as he asks for directions. His writing, however, carries the day. The *Times* continues to publish his weekly accounts, and he replaces Wayfarer as a pen name with Yeoman—the term for someone holding a small landed estate, evoking independent farmers as the moral backbone of a democratic nation.[18] His first-person reports prove successful enough that in 1856 he republishes his first dispatches as *A Journey in the Seaboard Slave States*—in hard covers and, for once, under his own name. *A Journey through Texas* appears in the following year. All this literary activity, exhausting but not lucrative, occurs in the years just before Frederick, in 1857, begins his difficult day job as park superintendent. Writing and revising will continue even while he supervises a large and sometimes restive workforce dominated by recent immigrants. He publishes a revised edition of *Walks and Talks* in 1859. By his mid-thirties, improbably, he is an established author.

Frederick, as a literary figure in New York City, adopts a dapper man-about-town look, which at least suggests that he can afford a new wardrobe. His monthly income and literary standing receive a boost when his father buys him a one-third partnership in the publishing house Dix, Edwards & Company. Dix Edwards, as the firm is called, pays Frederick a salary for editorial work—mostly on *Putnam's Monthly*, which it acquires from the enterprising but cash-strapped George Putnam. *Putnam's*, in contrast to its international rival *Harper's*, focuses on American writers, and Frederick as editor meets Emerson in Concord, helps oversee Melville's *Benito Cereno*, and rubs shoulders with the most popular poet in the English-speaking world, Henry Wadsworth Longfellow. The acclaimed British novelist William Makepeace Thackeray knows Frederick well enough to entertain him in London. These are heady, short-lived glory days before Dix Edwards abruptly goes belly up.

As the precarious house of writing crashes down around him, Frederick—despite his impressive credentials and connections—is left

Frederick Law Olmsted (c. 1860–1862). Courtesy of the National Park Service, Frederick Law Olmsted National Historic Site.

broke and stranded at Morris Cove wondering how to pay the innkeeper and what possibly comes next.

⁝⁝⁝

What comes next is a job at Central Park, although Frederick's success as a writer at first actually hurts his chances. His contemporaries are full of praise. James Russell Lowell writes that there is no more valuable contribution to American history than Olmsted's *A Journey in the Back Country* (1860). Charles Eliot Norton calls Olmsted's books "the most important contribution to an exact acquaintance with the conditions and result of slavery in this country that have ever been published."[19] *The Cotton Kingdom* (1861) lists among its English admirers Charles Darwin and John Stuart Mill. Praise doesn't pay the bills. When Dix Edwards fails in 1857, Frederick's one-third partnership is not only worthless but also entangles him in debt, as he feels obliged to repay his father's investment. It is in August 1857 that Frederick retreats to the Connecticut seaside inn to produce a few final yeoman-like dispatches. He owes $75 for three months' lodging, $60 total to a pair of friends, his shoes are worn out, and he is low on coal.[20] His vagabond, wayfaring journey may have reached the end of the road.

Charles Elliott, his companion for afternoon tea at Morris Cove, is a New York City businessman and vice president of the local Republican Party. A former Free-Soiler, he had once helped Frederick send the mountain howitzer to Kansas, and he had studied with Andrew Jackson Downing. Just four months earlier, he had also been appointed to the first Board of Commissioners for Central Park, and he knows that the board is looking to hire a park superintendent. It is Sunday, August 9, 1857. Does Frederick wish to apply? *Wonderful intricacy in the web*, as Emerson puts it. Frederick has no motive higher than simply applying for a job because he is broke and out of prospects. It is a world of unknowns. The debates over slavery are growing hotter. Abreast of his life, he boards the next steamer to New York City.

4

¦¦¦

A Young Snowy Owl

ON THE FIRST warm spring day after weeks of cold, gray, rainy skies, I'm drawn to the hillsides of Central Park along with hundreds of sunbathers suddenly sporting shorts and tank tops. On this particular day I celebrate by taking an unfamiliar shortcut home through the Ramble and its densely wooded tangle of uneven paths that Olmsted and Vaux regard as the visual highlight of the lower park. The Ramble almost invites you to get lost, or at least to lose your bearings until you stumble across a familiar path or glimpse a telltale skyscraper. It's where you muddle along, trusting that you won't get totally lost, just pleasantly confused perhaps, nodding to passersby who also look confused. Even the name *Ramble* acknowledges a pleasure in wandering, but I've made a very bad decision. The thick woods and humpbacked boulders turn the paths into obstacle courses. I'm starting down a few cement stairs when suddenly I trip.

I grab the handrail and hang on, upside down, dangling like a sloth. My shame masks the pain as more sure-footed fellow ramblers climb past me, most averting their eyes. Limping the mile home, I pretend that I'm not really hurt, although my right knee buckles when I get up from the sofa. I silently curse Frederick Law Olmsted, Calvert Vaux, and their booby-trapped fake wilderness.

Central Park, I'm thinking, set me up, luring me with the promise of a springtime stroll. I'd like to blame anything but inattentiveness, but I know that I took my eye off the stairs. Inattention is a bigger problem than I suspect. Calcutta-born writer Amitav Ghosh identifies it as an under-

33

lying pattern in the deadly string of floods, tornados, and firestorms that insurance companies still call acts of God. Ghosh argues that our current bizarre weather, unlike the climatic changes of prehistoric eras, is largely a human creation and that, deep down, most people know it. We repress the idea, of course, or deny it altogether, stuffing it into the black box of our unconscious minds, but the disasters just keep on coming, like uncanny visitations. "They are the mysterious work of our own hands," Ghosh writes in explanation, "returning to haunt us in unthinkable shapes and forms."[1]

What Ghosh describes is a globalized version of the unconscious process that Freud called the return of the repressed. We refuse to pay attention, we deny what we know deep down, and it comes back in malevolent shapes to haunt us. Did my fall result from simple inattention? Or does it resemble, in miniature, a wider inattention to our surroundings and to the natural world? Ghosh would say that, self-absorbed, we simply don't know where we're going. Climate change in any case has arrived in Central Park, even if in a slow-motion spread like an oil slick. There is of course so much that we don't notice. We don't notice the soil warming as spring arrives or how the air bears an invisible human signature in nanoparticles that show up in statistics about rising childhood asthma. Still, not all forms of inattention are equal, and I quickly reject the idea that my tumble is a return of whatever repressed desire drew me to a hillside spread with sunbathers.

Central Park as an astonishing green alternative to the grid of Manhattan cross streets poses a question that might well trip us up. What world and what legacy are we leaving—as our predecessors left us Central Park—for future generations? The uncanny orange haze that in 2023 enveloped New York City is in one sense completely natural, as southerly winds carry the smoke from Canadian wildfires. Authorities advise the vulnerable to stay indoors. Ghosh, in another sense, may be right. Humans have helped create the conditions that stoke the flames in ultra-dry forest canopies. Is global climate change, with its legacy of city-choking orange smoke, the gift we truly want to leave to future generations?

Central Park seems to exert almost a gravitational attraction, as if it has a direct line into the unconscious. Friends across the country tell me that they feel a personal connection to the park. Its uncanniness for me involves a forgetting so deep that I mostly forget that I've forgotten. My daily contacts with nature have dwindled to a walk in the park. Many people seem to compensate for a lost contact with house pets. Dogs are the most popular pets in the United States, occupying sixty-five million households. Cats come next, in forty-six million homes. Eleven million households, the outliers, are home to fish. In the United States, the total bill for pet ownership in 2022 amounts to $136.8 billion.[2] Real money invites an explanation about what people receive in return, especially companionship. Don't overthink it, I tell myself. Central Park is just a perfect place to walk the dog. Isn't there also, however, in every visit to the park, a dim contact with something we have lost and almost forgotten?

Loss is a complex state, as anyone knows who has lost someone they love. Edward O. Wilson in 1984 introduced the biophilia hypothesis, which holds that humans have an innate tendency to seek connections with nature.[3] "I long ago lost a hound, a bay horse, and a turtle dove," writes Thoreau in a famous passage from *Walden* (1854), "and I am still on their trail." He adds: "I have met one or two who had heard the hound, and the tramp of the horse, and even seen the dove disappear behind a cloud, and they seemed as anxious to recover them as if they had lost them themselves."[4] There is no evidence that Thoreau had lost an actual hound, horse, and turtle dove. As metaphors, however, and as representatives of the natural world, they evoke Freud's distinction, in *Mourning and Melancholia* (1917), between the loss of an object and the loss of something to which we cannot give a name. Parks, like pets, may reflect our affection for something we sense that we've lost but cannot name, perhaps because it refers to a lost contact with nature. Thoreau is not the only person, he points out, who seems to recognize the disappearing traces of what he has lost and, crucially, they share the sense of loss.

The magic of Central Park has sources that, for me, lie concealed in a mix of feelings that are more than personal. The endless benches start to fill up as soon as the park opens and begin to empty again as dusk falls in a human systole and diastole, as if it doesn't matter who sits on which bench, or whether they read the inscriptions on small rectangular plaques that mostly memorialize lost loved ones. People too, as many seem to forget, belong to the natural world, in which sense an entry into the park is a little like, without our conscious intention, coming home. Tourists, birdwatchers, and runners are as native here as the dogs, pigeons, and rodents, all members of one big extended family, so that Central Park offers more than a respite from the swarming cityscape that surrounds it. It is a place where we feel we belong.

Roy Rosenzweig and Elizabeth Blackmar, in their superb history *The Park and the People* (1992), provide an indispensable guide to the changing cast of characters whose voices fill the 843 acres and intervening years with a ghostly, inaudible soundtrack.[5] At ground level, the flat green rectangle seen from above turns into a three-dimensional mélange of people and nature buzzing with sound. Plays, concerts, and reunions mix with the shouts of children or the crack of a bat. Traces of previous generations are visible not just on the backs of benches or on the historical markers. Dogs, carrying the history of their human-shaped breeds, almost outnumber their less purebred owners. I've seen dog walkers hold the leashes to half a dozen large poodles or setters that look suspiciously like first cousins. The undoglike calm of most New York City dogs never fails to amaze me.

▦

A rare snowy owl arrives unannounced in Central Park on January 27, 2021. UFOs might have caused less fuss. All of New York City seems to know within hours. Her age and gender are clear from the dark-tipped feathers curving in symmetrical bands, except around her eyes, beak, and talons. Owls are reputed wise, but this youngster looks spiffed up and ready to party, although maybe unsure exactly where the party is. Meanwhile, the Manhattan Bird Alert notifies its 38,000 followers, so a party of sorts does indeed break out. The *New York Times* sends a reporter. A rare owl is news fit to print. Central Park hosted its last snowy owl in 1890, when a whole flock landed on their annual migratory route, doubtless a case of owl inattention.

The lone snowy owl that arrives in 2021 perhaps took a wrong turn over Nova Scotia. Too late. Cameras click, with one enterprising photographer even launching a drone. "The owl was aware of it," says a Parks Department ranger: "It was stressing it out."[6] A hobby-size drone once hovered outside my hotel window, blades whirring, and I didn't like it either. Several big crows hop by, menacingly. How do these angry city-slicker crows know that snowy owls hunt crows? Humans have an inborn fear of snakes and spiders too, which suggests an ancient genetic origin. It's certain that these crows, at least as it applies to snowy owls, don't buy into biophilia. Just then a territorial red-tailed hawk swoops past, also annoyed. Word has spread in birdland almost as fast as on social media. "Seeing the snowy owl is like winning the lottery," says Molly Adams, an experienced Audubon Society

A young female snowy owl. Courtesy of Kevin Vande Vusse.

outreach manager with no inborn animus. Another lost Arctic snowy owl turns up in 2023 east of Los Angeles. "It's a bird I never expected to see in my lifetime," one Angeleno declares, "and here it is right in front of me. I did a little happy dance."[7]

▪▪▪

Global climate change is disrupting migratory patterns, which can't fully explain why a lost snowy owl can send sophisticated city-dwellers into a frenzy. The love of nature also seems connected with its opposite. It is psychoanalyst Erich Fromm who first introduces the term *biophilia*, describing it as "the passionate love of life and of all that is alive."[8] Fromm's account, however, appears in a thick tome entitled *The Anatomy of Human Destructiveness* (1973). Perhaps psychoanalysis can explain the apparently equally strong human desire to shoot up or blow up or pave over so much of the natural world. Prizes used to be awarded every Christmas in Central Park to hunters who bagged the most birds.

Central Park has been a haven for birdwatchers ever since the first census in 1886 counted 121 different species.[9] Every Christmas since 1900 the Audubon Society repeats an annual bird count—wildly unscientific, since bad weather often depletes the number of volunteers. Central Park turns out to be a vital rest stop or oasis (stocked with berries, seeds, and insects) along the migratory Atlantic Flyway that stretches from Greenland to South America. The young snowy owl carries bad news. "Nearly 3 Billion Birds Gone since 1970," reads one headline.[10] The bird population in North America today is down by 2.9 billion breeding adults; forests have lost 1 billion birds; grassland populations have declined by 53 percent. The numbers are bad too in the United Kingdom, where forty million birds have disappeared since 1970.[11] Birds remain a potent symbol of the wild—*free as a bird*, the saying goes—which suggests why we civilized folks get so excited about an occasional exotic visitor from the disappearing wild kingdom.

New Yorkers seem almost elated when a Eurasian eagle-owl escapes after vandals damage its enclosure at the Central Park Zoo. Flaco, as he or she is known, manages to survive for over a year perched on Manhattan rooftops and water towers. One night in 2024 on the Upper West Side Flaco slams full speed into a building. One more corpse among the 230,000 birds similarly killed each year in New York City.[12]

The most famous avian visitor is doubtless a red-tailed hawk that in 1991 builds a nest in the facade of an apartment building on Fifth Avenue directly across from Central Park.[13] Pale Male—the media nickname—also runs into trouble from territorial crows that refuse a nesting permit in the park. Humans, however, are fascinated. A webcam captures every paradoxical moment of a wild hawk nesting on the chic Upper East Side. Pale Male quickly attracts groupies, a documentary filmmaker, and feature writers. Several books attest to his rock-star status, which he confirms by fathering some thirty chicks. Latchkey red-tailed hawks are now a common sight in Central Park, where the local squirrels, pigeons, and rats provide a

Pale Male. Jeremy Seto, CC BY-SA 2.0, via Wikimedia Commons.

steady diet. The public excitement suggests that more is at stake than the sighting of anonymous wildlife. "I was thrilled," says David Barrett, creator of the Manhattan Bird Alert, when in January 2024 he spots the return of a familiar bald eagle that also bears a human nickname: "this had to be Rover!"[14] Birds are rovers, powerful icons (as humans imagine) of freedom and wildness.

"In Wildness is the preservation of the world," writes Thoreau.[15] He is five years older than Olmsted, and Olmsted as editor acquires an essay by Thoreau for *Putnam's Monthly*. Although they share an affection for the natural world, the extreme value that Thoreau attributes to Wildness—with a capital letter—differs from Olmsted's emphasis on parks as a civilizing force. Thoreau distinguishes carefully between wildness and wilderness. Wilderness is external, the name for largely untamed terrain, whereas wildness is largely an untamed internal quality. Wilderness even in Thoreau's day is rapidly disappearing. He lives in a small New England town where he helps in the family-run pencil business. "I have traveled a great deal in Concord," he writes, savoring the irony of excursions that never leave home. Wildness, however, is all around. He finds it in the springtime frolic of livestock and in the rich muck at the bottom of a bog. He also honors a wildness that humans carry within, no matter how sophisticated or domesticated we are. It is wildness that not only survives the loss of wilderness but also, Thoreau writes, holds a power to preserve the world.

Olmsted and Vaux in Central Park create in the Ramble a deliberate simulation of wilderness, but otherwise emphasize a picturesque landscape with, as they believe, a civilizing moral power: a force to tame the raw, crude, or wild impulses associated with the lower classes. Parks, in Olmsted's view, thus endorse the values of the gentlemanly order to which he belongs. Pastoral scenery, he believes, holds the vital power to transform raw immigrants into orderly citizens. It actively eradicates wildness and disorderly behavior, with which he has firsthand experience and no sympathy. The financial downturn in November 1857 creates an ugly scene after he earns the board's permission to hire and fire workers. He is making his way, undetected, through a crowd of some two thousand angry and desperate immigrants as an orator on a wagon urges them to demand that Frederick hire them. If he refuses? Frederick watches as the orator holds up a rope and points to a nearby tree. The crowd cheers.[16]

Urban parks, Olmsted later emphasizes, can exert a refining influence on the people, by whom he often means immigrants, whose rough edges conceal the threat of violence. "He felt it his duty as a gentleman," Rosenzweig and Blackmar conclude, "to train the poor and the uneducated, whom he did not entirely trust, in the tastes and manners he had inherited. He shared with members of the park board the concept of stewardship that assumed that they knew what was best for the people."[17] Olmsted also, however, values the preservation of what Thoreau called wilderness. He is later appointed to write a plan and charter for Yosemite, creating an intellectual foundation for the world's first system of national parks.[18] Central Park meanwhile contains at least a reminder of what cities have threatened to eradicate. "The design in planting the Ramble has been to give, if possible, the delicate flavor of wildness," writes art critic Clarence Cook in 1869, perhaps less careful than Thoreau in his usage, "so hard to seize and imprison when civilization has once put it to flight."[19]

Esau, inheriting the eldest son's biblical claim to precedence, famously sells his birthright for a single meal of lentil stew (Genesis 25:34). "I trust that I shall never thus sell my birthright for a mess of pottage," Thoreau writes, referring to his inheritance of wildness.[20] Birds—or at least certain charismatic birds—are linked not only to ideas of wildness but also to traditions of beauty, spirit, and power. "When thou seest an Eagle," writes poet William Blake, "thou seest a portion of Genius, lift up thy head!"[21] From Native American headdresses to Easter bonnets, the complex social history of avian feathers offers its own slant on the human desire for images of beauty, spirit, and power. Central Park, from its initial funding in 1853 through its continuing allure on the first warm spring day, expresses a tacit multigenerational desire to reassert a birthright that connects us to the natural world. The birthright may be misplaced, displaced, sold, or forgotten at times, but never entirely expunged. Central Park implicitly affirms that our ancient attachment to nature and to its wildness is as elemental as love or pain.

Two hours ago, nursing my injured knee as I gaze into the dense green upper canopy, I glimpse a bright red flash. I hobble for the binoculars. Is it what I suspect? The seventh-floor window offers an ideal vantage. Migrant birds are especially vulnerable to climate change, and loons sometimes fall from the sky encased in ice. False springs, increasingly common, trap the migrating birds in sudden, atypical winter storms.[22] Adjusting the focus, I recognize the jet-black wings and deep-red body. I check my *Field Guide*. Yes! Except for my right knee, which is still throbbing, I could almost do a little happy dance. A scarlet tanager!

5

An Unpractical Man

FREDERICK'S LITERARY REPUTATION almost sinks his chances for the job as park superintendent. What does a writer and editor know about clearing out piggeries, draining swamps, and uprooting brush? The assumption that he lacks practical skills rankles Olmsted for the rest of his life. Self-defensive to a fault, he turns prickly whenever he feels disrespected, especially in practical matters. He not only carries a grudge but waits to spring his revenge. The extended autobiographical fragment that he writes late in his life is titled, aggressively, "Passages in the Life of an Unpractical Man."[1]

The era of climate change coincides with the rise of experts. Certificates, degrees, résumés, honors, and track records are necessities of professional life. Licensed employment agencies openly state that the unqualified need not apply. Charles Elliott, perhaps triangulated through Andrew Downing, clearly believes that Olmsted possesses the necessary practical skills, but others know him only by reputation as a literary man. The Board of Commissioners sees the park superintendent as merely an interim, low-level employee overseeing cleanup operations: "a sort of glorified foreman."[2] Egbert Ludovicus Viele, the chief engineer to whom the newly hired superintendent will report, contemptuously and specifically refers to Olmsted as an *unpractical* man.

Not *practical*? "There was not an operation in progress on the park in which I had not considerable personal experience," Olmsted later insists.[3] Didn't he plant five thousand fruit tree saplings on Tosomock Farm *with his own hands*? Hasn't he learned basic surveying with a civil engineer, worked on the farm of noted agricultural reformer George Geddes, and received informal training in horticulture from the great Andrew Jackson Downing? He talks drains with the figure whom he calls "the head working-gardener" at Birkenhead Park, and he installs similar drains at Tosomock Farm, even helping to secure new tile-making machinery for the county agricultural society. (He and engineer George Waring, Jr. will later install some sixty miles of tile drains under Central Park.)[4] His travel through lawless and hostile regions is no occupation for the faint-hearted. He and his brother John begin their journey through west Texas by purchasing a double-barreled shotgun, a single-shot breech-loading rifle, several Colt revolvers, and hunting knives advertised as good for "fighting."[5]

The plot thickens and the pace quickens after Olmsted hears about his apparent lack of qualifications. He works fast—an enduring trait—and three days after taking tea with Charles Elliott at Morris Cove he has rounded up multiple endorsements and submitted impressive letters to the board in support of his application.

The politics of global climate change can seem intractable because there are so many competing stakeholders. The nineteenth-century origin of Central Park, while hardly a legitimate comparison, is similar in one respect. No important action succeeds in New York City politics-free—and little that is unimportant. Carmine DeSapio, the last boss of the Tammany Hall political machine, once opened up City Hall on a Saturday so that my father could retrieve my birth certificate. Tammany Hall also controls the Democratic Party's patronage system that operates in full force as Olmsted submits his application. Luckily, he is viewed as moderate, disengaged from party politics. Elliott describes him to the narrowly divided board as a Republican whom Democrats can live with. It is, however, a delicate dance. Olmsted's application contains the signatures of some two hundred supporters, some from his heyday at Dix Edwards, including celebrities such as William Cullen Bryant and Washington Irving. Irving, then in his seventies, helps rally seven more prominent New Yorkers. Frederick is at least overqualified in the practical art of rounding up referees.

Frederick believes that Irving's endorsement is what "turned the balance," as he writes later.[6] The board takes an unusually long time in deciding, which suggests debate and possible deadlock. At last, minus only a puff of white smoke, the board announces its decision to hire Olmsted as park superintendent. Frederick swallows his pride over the issue of salary. The board first had set the salary at $3,000 per year but then, without explanation, cuts it in half. Frederick is in no position to negotiate. As he writes to his father, in a question that implies no burning desire for a career in landscape design: "What else can I do for a living?"[7]

∷

Indirection, as Frederick's early life suggests, is sometimes the best way to find your destined path. *A Journey in the Seaboard Slave States* (1856) is the first work in which pen names and anonymity are replaced by his now-familiar triplet signature, Frederick Law Olmsted. James Hamilton in a supporting petition had identified him to the board simply as "Mr. F. Law Olmsted," at least stripped of any literary flourish. His petition also pointedly mentions Frederick's "practical training as an agriculturalist."[8] His experience at Tosomock Farm, however, fails to impress Frederick's hard-nosed boss at Central Park, the mustachioed chief engineer Egbert Ludovicus Viele. *Vee-lay*, as he pronounces his surname, is an ambitious veteran of the Mexican-American War. His pyramid-shaped mausoleum at West Point, guarded by a pair of marble sphinxes, reflects his outsized ego while extending his practicality even beyond the grave. He thus installs a buzzer in his coffin wired to the main office in case of an inadvertent live burial. Battle-seasoned, he swears like a trooper, and he assumes that it will be easy to scare off the unwanted and impractical travel-writing dandy who arrives for a courtesy call dressed like a gentleman. Viele instructs a young foreman to lead Olmsted on an immediate tour of the park, through sloughs brimming with "black and unctuous slime," as Olmsted describes it, where at times he sinks "nearly half leg deep."[9] A Democrat, Viele has stocked the workforce with idlers whom Olmsted rightly suspects are political cronies: "Wood Democrats," hired as followers of their Tammany Hall patron, Mayor Fernando Wood. Olmsted shrugs off the slime. Fearless and impossible to intimidate, he has waded through bogs far worse on Tosomock Farm.

A gift for improvisation and an instinct for seizing opportunities prove highly desirable in facing the unknown. Central Park, despite its familiar sloughs, is a realm of the unknown. Olmsted doesn't know, of course, that Central Park will rearrange his life. He doesn't know that Viele has previously won over a rump subset of commissioners to approve his design for the eventual park. He doesn't even know Calvert Vaux, although they had met briefly at Andrew Downing's firm. The unpractical man, however, quickly masters the art of site preparation. He initially directs some seven

General Egbert L. Viele (between 1860 and 1870). Library of Congress.

View of house and surrounding fields. New York Public Library Digital Collections.

hundred workers who cart off rock, drain the bogs, root out underbrush tangled with poison ivy, and tear down outbuildings. A photo shows a well-kept vegetable garden, likely German, beside a tumbledown shack that looks ready to self-destruct, with a new park pavilion visible in the distance. Soon the pavilion too will disappear as the park continues to change. Change is the bedrock of Central Park.

Change is also basic to Olmsted's character as expressed in his ability to shift course, to seize opportunities, and to improvise. The park bears his signature. Modest in stature, five feet seven, he cuts a commanding figure, even dictatorial some say. He also inspires loyalty for his tireless work ethic. A colleague later describes him, not entirely in admiration, as possessing a "monomania for system and organization."[10] The board quickly recognizes his practical skills and, as he asks, authorizes him to fire idlers, malingerers, and incompetents. Within a year of starting, he can write to his father: "I have got the park into a capital discipline, a perfect system, working like a machine."[11]

∷

Melioration, writes Emerson in *The Conduct of Life* (1860), "is the law of nature." Men are valued, he adds, "precisely as they exert onward or meliorating force." A failure to improve the self or the world he describes as "the only mortal distemper."[12] Distemper as a highly contagious disease of dogs suggests how deeply Emerson is committed to melioration as a defining human virtue. Olmsted, beyond practical, is also a born improver, an inspired pragmatist, evident early when he had transformed a farmyard puddle into an ornamental water feature. His pragmatism taps into an American tradition that leads from Benjamin Franklin to William James. While he shares Emerson's passion for the material world of corn and melons, his meliorating practice resists a drift into Emersonian realms of the transcendental. After an early brush with religion as a young man, he comes to regard theological debates as a waste of time. He says that when other people go to church on Sunday, he eats a larger than usual breakfast, reads two newspapers, and smokes a cigar.

His pragmatic streak, while it favors Sunday cigars, does not provide immunity from loss, melancholy, or anguish. Continuing financial worries and professional anxieties coincide with his bouts of serious illness, including depression.[13] Still, he tries to meliorate even his relationship with Viele, forwarding to his father Viele's request for a London overcoat in "nice, thin, light, silk faced, English India rubber."[14] Viele's duties as chief engineer include creating a topographical map of the site, and he regards himself as the obvious choice to design the new park, since he already has a plan on file. He has no reason to fear a rival—certainly not his "literary" subordinate, who has no experience in park design. Viele is likely surprised, but not dismayed, when the board on October 13, 1857, announces its decision to hold an open international competition for the design of Central Park. He will simply submit his former plan.

Calvert Vaux deserves credit for persuading the board to hold an open competition. He also deserves credit for persuading Olmsted to join him in creating what they come to call the Greensward plan. Olmsted at first demurs, perhaps in deference to Viele, but also knowing that he has no formal training in landscape design. He knows something now about site preparation, but he is still engaged in writing and is wholly unqualified to design a massive urban park. Viele will pop up later, with the resilience of a cartoon villain, to file a lawsuit claiming that Olmsted and Vaux have stolen his design. Viele, to his credit, at least knows the terrain. His *Sanitary & Topographical Map of the City and Island of New York* (1865) charts the streams, marshes, and coastline in relation to the street grid, and it is still in use today. He loses his post as chief engineer after Olmsted and Vaux win the design competition. In a final twist, however, the wily and resourceful Viele manages in 1884 to engineer his election as president of New York City's Department of Public Parks, which puts Central Park once more under his command.

It is late November 1857, after Frederick begins his job as superintendent and has the park working like a machine, but there is trouble ahead. His beloved brother John has shared two long excursions as his trusted companion, including the risky trip through Texas. Despite steadily worsening health, John edits the manuscript for *A Journey through Texas* (1857), relieving Frederick of one extra burden, and John likely even writes some of the text, working from Frederick's notes. Tuberculosis, however, has dug its claws into his lungs, and soon he decides to travel abroad in the nineteenth-century ritual search for a healthier climate, along with his wife, Mary, and their three young children. John dies abroad at age thirty-two, on November 24, 1857. Frederick, distraught, loses more than a travel companion, an editor, and a trusted source of emotional support. You have lost not only a brother, his father writes to him, a little sharply, but also "almost your only friend."[15]

Melioration has its limits, and practical skills cannot repair every loss. John sends a last dying letter from France that concludes, in shaky handwriting, with a charge that Frederick cannot ignore: "Don't let Mary suffer while you are alive."[16]

6

###

Enter Calvert Vaux

CALVERT VAUX WOULD MAKE an unlikely American hero even if he weren't born in London, short of stature, bohemian, eccentric, artistic, and without prospects when, at twenty-six, he leaps at the invitation in 1850 to join Andrew Downing in his Newburgh landscape firm. Downing clearly sees something exceptional in Vaux beyond his watercolors (then on display in London) and beyond his ability to write very fast backward. Engravers must inscribe any verbal text in mirror image, and his skill in writing backward earns Vaux a precarious freelance income engraving text for map publishers after a less than productive architectural apprenticeship. He travels to New York and never looks back.

He also in effect rescues Olmsted, twice, ultimately eclipsing his own architectural contributions at Central Park as he sets his wandering career-challenged partner on the path to become "Landscape Architect for the Nation."[1]

Vaux and Olmsted, despite their differences, are born risk-takers. They also share a firm belief in democratic values. The abrupt transatlantic move that brings Vaux to Newburgh suggests a discontent with the class-bound hierarchies of Victorian England. Six years after his arrival he becomes an American citizen, in 1856, and he remains a passionate advocate for republican virtues. In fact, he openly but mildly criticizes the value that Olmsted places on gentlemanly status, preferring the company of artists and artisans, including painters. His rapid rise to partner means that when

Calvert Vaux (c. 1865–1871). Courtesy of the Museum of the City of New York.

Downing drowns in 1852 Vaux takes over the firm, and thereafter he increasingly accepts commissions in New York City. He moves there in 1856 with his bride of two years, the sister of painter Jervis McEntee, a sometime member of the Hudson River School. Over the coming decades Vaux shuttles among artists, architects, and a clientele of social elites in New York City. There, as a sure sign of esteem, he is chosen to design the Metropolitan Museum of Art when it moves in 1880 to its present location within the park. His story belongs to an archetypal American narrative, but it differs from both the Horatio Alger paradigm of rags-to-riches and the immigrant's vision of America as the land of (vague) opportunities. He lives by a specific subset of skills and powers valued by the ancient Greeks when they personified Opportunity as an Olympian god.

Opportunity differs from luck, which philosopher Martha Nussbaum defines as whatever just *happens*, wherever, whenever. Opportunity doesn't just happen but *arises* at distinctive moments, as suggested by its Latin etymology referring to the arrival of a ship at port. Luck is notoriously fickle—luck runs out, you can't ever count on it—whereas opportunity implies that people can shape their own lives with the right timely action. Ancient Greeks who puzzled over luck and fate thus assigned a special god to personify opportunity. Kairos, the god of opportunity, occupies an honored place among the Olympian deities as the youngest son of Zeus. His name in Greek means, literally, "the right moment."[2]

The right moment in Greek philosophical thought evokes images from archery and weaving. The arrow and the shuttle must be launched at exactly the right and only moment that assures success. Kairos in effect embraces the instinct, training, skill, and timing required to sense the right moment. Ancient statues of Kairos always include a double set of wings: larger angel-like wings on his upper back and smaller wings on his heels. With a double set of wings, Kairos is very fast, like the fleeting opportunities that come and go. He also sports a distinctive haircut: entirely bald, except for a large forelock over his brow. The meaning? You must seize Kairos by the forelock, as soon as he approaches, or you miss your chance. Lightning fast, Kairos is gone in an instant. Once slipped past, as the bald pate of Kairos suggests, missed opportunities leave you with nothing to hold onto.

The art of the right moment requires speed and judgment as well as skill and intuition: the knowledge *when* to grab the forelock and the quickness to grab it. Like Vaux when Downing offers him a job, you don't have weeks to weigh the pros and cons. When the moment is right, you must act fast and take your shot.

Vaux lives by an intuitive art of the right moment. Only eight years old when his father dies, he survives by his wits with a bohemian nonchalance. After completing his apprenticeship to an aged icon of the Gothic Revival, he leaves on a walking tour of the Continent, much like Olmsted but without a wealthy father to underwrite the costs. Affable and gifted at working behind the scenes, he inspires an easy confidence among his important clients. These same clients, after he moves to New York City in 1856, might well inform him about Viele's design for Central Park, which he also could have found himself in the *First Annual Report on the Improvement of the Central Park* (dated January 1, 1857), which "contained a lithograph of Mr. Viele's plan," according to Clarence Cook and which Cook, an art critic by profession, dismisses as "a matter-of-fact, tasteless affair as is always produced by engineers."[3] It is primarily Vaux—a tribute to his social skills and to his behind-the-scenes deftness—who helps persuade the Board of Commissioners to shelve Viele's plan as lacking what he calls "artistic" merit and to hold an open international competition.

Olmsted in starting his new position as superintendent in late 1857 remains aloof from park politics. His day job pays the rent, which lets him continue with the important work of writing. While Olmsted supervises by day and writes by night, however, Vaux finds exactly the right life-changing moment to intervene. He invites Olmsted to collaborate on a park design for the open competition. Olmsted delays, but he too must sense that the moment is right. Kairos brings them together in a collaboration for the ages. It takes years before Olmsted clearly and openly confesses his massive debt to Vaux. In his seventies he explains to a journalist who plans to write an article that celebrates his long career, "I should have had nothing to do with the design of the Central Park, or of Prospect Park, had not Vaux invited me to join him in those works."[4] The right moment to make this admission apparently didn't arrive until his career is almost over, but when it arrives Olmsted couldn't be clearer about his debt to Vaux.

"But for his invitation," he continues, "I should not have been a landscape architect. I should have been a farmer."[5]

I'm not proud of it, but online real estate is my guilty pleasure, despite a personal history of buying high and selling low. I seem to possess a knack for missing the right moment. The fantasy of finding an affordable stone cottage along the Hudson River, maybe even in Newburgh, keeps me surfing the Internet at odd hours, and one day I notice an old, dark gray two-story clapboard house not far from Newburgh, in nearby Kingston. The house, almost the opposite of a charming stone cottage, looks as if it belongs in a horror flick. The floor plan, if not spooky, is distinctly odd and includes a large second living room upstairs with a ceiling that extends up to the exposed rafters. The overview says the house was "built and designed by famed Central Park architect Calvert Vaux in the 1890s."

I'm hooked. Is this the right moment to buy? I decide to wait and do some research. The house, as it turns out, wasn't exactly "built and designed" by Vaux but rather it "contains" an artist's studio that Vaux designed in 1854. I discover that Vaux was pleased enough with the studio—designed for his brother-in-law Jervis McEntee in the village of Rondout with views of the Catskill Mountains—that in 1857 he included the design in a book meant to attract new clients, *Villas and Cottages*. His illustration of the studio emphasizes a key point for Vaux: buildings must harmonize with the environment. Surrounded by artful plantings, the studio blends in with its semirural setting, which includes not only the distant mountains but also, as in a picturesque painting, village steeples nearby. Domestic architecture, he writes, needs to consider "the climate, the soil, the length of day, the wants of the people, [and] the habit and form of government."[6]

Calvert Vaux, *Design for an Artist's Studio*. From Calvert Vaux, *Villas and Cottages*, 2nd ed. (New York: Harper and Brothers, 1864).

Soon I solve the mystery of the upstairs living room. When McEntee no longer used the studio, a relative moved it to the family property close by in Kingston, where it was recycled as the top floor of the historic clapboard house that I decided to pass on.

Calvert Vaux, or at least his reputation, in some sense shares the fate of his studio: swallowed up and incorporated within a larger structure. Well aware of the overshadowing, he resents Olmsted's focus on administration or management as more vital than artistic vision to the creation of Central Park. He later reproves his partner for leaving the "big job of the art" unfinished, as if Central Park were no more than "an ornament among many ornaments in the watch chain of F.L.O."[7] Full credit, of course, extends to many others, such as the Austrian head gardener, Ignaz Pilat, and British architect and polymath Jacob Wrey Mould, who helps design not only Belvedere Castle but also a trolley shelter at Eighth Avenue that makes the park far more accessible to everyday New Yorkers.[8] Vaux never slights Olmsted's genius, but he also emphasizes an alternative vision in which landscape and architecture harmonize, together embodying the ideals of a democratic union. Allegiance to the political values of his adopted country—basic to the creation of Central Park—underlies his insistence on what he calls the "republican art idea."[9]

"We have listened too long to the courtly muses of Europe," writes Emerson in "The American Scholar" (1837), a cultural declaration of independence.[10] Andrew Downing shares an Emersonian sense that America requires its own republican arts, free from royal courts and aristocratic estates. This widely shared political vision underlies Vaux's dedication of *Villas and Cottages* to "Caroline E. Downing, and to the Memory of her husband, Andrew J. Downing." Vaux, however, quickly hires another British architect trained in the Gothic Revival, Frederick Withers, when he takes over Downing's firm, and the links between Central Park and Anglo-European traditions are nowhere more evident than in the painterly theory and practice in landscape art known as "the picturesque."

The raging popularity of picturesque scenery did not depend on clear definitions. "There are few words whose meaning has been less accurately determined than that of the word Picturesque," writes the influential British theorist Uvedale Price.[11] *Picturesque*, however vague, refers specifically to the pictorial style associated with painters Salvator Rosa in Italy and Claude Lorrain in France. Their shaggy foliage, dappled shadows, ragged terrain, and irregular textures create a recognizable aesthetic of contrast and variety. William Gilpin, another influential eighteenth-century British theorist, sums up the picturesque in his own irregular staccato prose: "We seek it among all the ingredients of landscape—trees—rocks— broken-grounds—woods—rivers—lakes—plains—vallies—mountains— and distances. These objects in themselves produce infinite variety."[12]

Infinite variety, for Vaux, is almost a synonym for the American natural landscape, and the picturesque style constitutes almost a native political aesthetic when translated onto American soil. Unlike typical scenes of power and vastness associated with the sublime, as in endless paintings of Niagara Falls and the Grand Canyon, picturesque landscapes invoke softer, more domestic scenes in which variety evokes a meditative calm— pastoral, rural, bucolic—possessing its own limitless inner dimension. Olmsted and Vaux share a commitment to picturesque design as appropriate for a park, especially where the landscape inspires a calm and contemplative quality. Olmsted's commitment to the picturesque extends even to his advanced age when he creates at Harvard the nation's first academic program in landscape architecture. He sends students to study Gilpin and Price as seriously, he writes in a letter, as "a student of Law would read Blackstone."[13]

Olmsted, despite has abiding respect for Gilpin and Price, comes to modify his views on the picturesque style as appropriate for urban parks. Olmsted tells an audience in 1870 that "very rugged ground, abrupt eminences, and what is technically called picturesque in distinction from merely beautiful or simply pleasing scenery is not the most desirable for a town park. Decidedly not in my opinion." He is now speaking as a newly minted authority on urban parks. "The park should, as far as possible, complement the town," he argues, emphasizing the contrast between parks and towns. "Openness is the one thing you cannot get in buildings."[14] Openness as an aesthetic ideal becomes increasingly important for Olmsted. The openness of urban parks, in contrast to the closure of cities and buildings, holds an almost spiritual beauty. "It should be the beauty," he informs his audience, "of the fields, the meadow, the prairie, of the green pastures, and the still waters." *Still waters*, in its allusion to the Twenty-Third Psalm, endows the openness of urban parks with an unspoken, secular *amen,* and it is also a belated *amen* that never interrupts the earlier astonishing collaboration that, despite their differences, he maintains with Calvert Vaux in their joint work at Central Park.

Collaborations as a creative endeavor distinct from the standard focus on individual achievement seem to be inherently unstable. Think of Steve Jobs and Steve Wozniak or—surnames sufficient—Astaire and Rogers, Pippen and Jordan, or Lennon and McCartney. Olmsted and Vaux do not exactly trip off the tongue as a similarly inseparable duo, but theirs is an inspired partnership, and their differences prove complementary, at least for a time. They need each other. Olmsted knows nothing about architecture and has only an amateur interest in art. Vaux is an expat Brit and knows little to nothing about the terrain proposed for Central Park. Except for a passing acquaintance through Downing, they barely know each other. Still, they spend almost every evening in Vaux's apartment on Eighteenth Street working on a submission for the Central Park design competition. The final date for submissions is April 1, 1858. There is still time to seize the opportunity.

Their collaboration hints at a significant countertradition in American life that exists alongside rugged individualism. Vaux, no mere sidekick, shares a vision with Olmsted in which their design will depend on a mutual respect for the natural terrain. "Nature first, 2nd and 3rd—Architecture after a while," he writes.[15] Architecture, however, also remains fundamental to Central Park. Bow Bridge, for example, is almost a visual metaphor of the Olmsted-Vaux collaboration. A photograph from 1860 shows far more than a decorative shortcut for pedestrians crossing the water. Commissioner Robert J. Dillon had proposed a suspension bridge with projecting towers, which Olmsted argues would interrupt the flow of the landscape, so Vaux designs only the second cast-iron bridge in America: an engineering and aesthetic triumph. Its graceful geometric arc accentuates the irregularities of the terrain to create perhaps the most photographed site in Central Park. It creates a welcome contrast in winter when it interrupts the stark monotone of snow, and it may even appear to overcome Olmsted's rigid contrast between parks and buildings. The twin towers of the San Remo apartments, designed by acclaimed architect Emery Roth and completed in 1930, now seem to rise over Bow Bridge—similar in coloration and style—like a visual extension of the park.

Central Park owes much to Vaux. He creates twenty-seven bridges and arches between 1859 and 1866, some with his assistant Jacob Wrey Mould, and the number eventually rises to more than thirty—each different and uniquely ornamented, built from brick, granite, marble, cast iron, rustic

Bow Bridge, Central Park (c. 1860). Royal Institute of British Architects.

wood, and rusticated gneiss boulders.[16] The materials vary in part because of economies instituted by Olmsted's nemesis Andrew Haswell Green, in his role as comptroller, but Vaux is already committed to variety as an aesthetic principle. His contributions are designed to blend with the landscape, not stand apart for attention, and their function is not simply to solve a specific architectural or structural problem but rather to express a human presence within the natural world. Vaux designs using varied geometrical features and diverse materials "to prevent monotony," he writes, but whatever prevents monotony also enhances variety. A monotone in its singleness is also the mortal foe of whatever comes forth from the complementary give-and-take of a collaborative relation.[17]

Not all collaborations are deliberate or official. Central Park would not exist without the contribution of various colorful, half-forgotten characters. Fernando Wood, for example, the wealthy Quaker regarded as the most corrupt mayor ever of New York City, which is saying something, intervened in March 1855 to veto a measure by the Board of Aldermen that would have shrunk the park by about one third. General Daniel E. Sickles, who among his political feats robs a US post office to prevent a rival from mailing circulars, regarded himself as "the Founder of Central Park"—referring to his secret machinations that extend to assuring the appointment of a judge whom he knew would approve the all-important report on payments to dispossessed landowners by the Commission of Estimate and Assessment.[18]

Successful collaborations are rare, since they depend in part on the unusual convergence of people with complementary talents. They also depend, crucially, on the art of the right moment: on risk-takers willing to seize the opportunities. The fit of temperaments needed for successful long-term relationships is not always possible in collaborations. Vaux, mild-mannered and accommodating in public, is a powerhouse behind the scenes. Olmsted, pragmatic in public as a disciplined, no-nonsense administrator, is scrappy in private and easily offended.[19] "Frederick the Great, Prince of the Park Police" is how Vaux in a rare moment of irritation refers to Olmsted's authoritarian tendencies.[20] They survive their differences and moments of friction because they need and respect each other, later maintaining for years an equal partnership in the landscape firm that bears their names.

Unfortunately, although working tirelessly at night and on weekends to create the extensive, innovative document to submit into competition embodying their design for Central Park, they miss the deadline. The right moment apparently has come and gone.

7

⣿

The Weeping Time

SORROW AND SUFFERING take on a personal dimension as Olmsted begins work on Central Park. The death of his brother John in November 1857 is a mighty blow, carrying with it the plea that Frederick cannot ignore: not to let Mary suffer.

Mary, not one to romanticize suffering, marries Frederick in June 1859. Families stuck together then. My great-grandfather, after his longtime wife Hattie dies, marries her sister Mattie. Mary reverses the pattern of disappointed courtships that marks Frederick's early years, and she provides a loving center for his vagabond career even after, at fifty, he relocates the family landscape business to Boston. Her support receives long overdue recognition in Gail Ward Olmsted's historical novel *Landscape of a Marriage* (2021), as Mary anchors their mobile lives, bears Frederick four children, helps as amanuensis, and protects his legacy during the sad final days when he suffers from dementia. Indeed, suffering and sorrow are inescapable as Frederick, Mary, and her three children take up residence on the northernmost grounds of Central Park.

Suffering is also in the air as the nation continues to learn about the horrors facing enslaved blacks. Theatergoers throng to emotional stage versions of *Uncle Tom's Cabin* (1852), the book that Abraham Lincoln in a famous quip to Stowe implies has caused the Civil War. The opposition to slavery is mixed with politics and, even in New York City, far from monolithic. Olmsted's dispatches home under the pen name Yeoman contain troubling glimpses that debunk the myth of Southern gentility, but many

New Yorkers resist abolition and oppose Lincoln, boycotting his stopover en route to his first inauguration. Political and economic anxieties run high. Mayor Fernando Wood seriously proposes, in January 1861, that New York secede from the Union and declare itself an unaffiliated free city. Few families North or South can escape personal suffering when open civil war breaks out in April 1861. Central Park emerges in a dark time of trauma, personal and national.

Olmstead in writing on the South doesn't highlight suffering, unlike Stowe. His opposition to slavery focuses on its weakness as an economic system, and his personal encounters with enslaved, freed, or escaped blacks are quite limited. In fact, Northerners have multiple reasons to discount black suffering. Minstrel shows are wildly popular in Northern cities, with white actors in blackface entertaining audiences with supposedly comic representations of enslaved blacks. Jim Crow is a standard ragtag figure from minstrel shows long before the name gets applied to laws enforcing racial segregation. Doctors meanwhile claim in medical journals that blacks do not feel pain—or at least far less pain than whites—which justifies a string of brutal human experiments. Such contradictions and absurdities fuel the daily passions as Frederick, promoted to architect-in-chief in 1858, pursues work on Central Park. It is unlikely he missed the *New-York Daily Tribune* in 1859 when it provides a full-page account of a particularly horrific episode: the largest known auction of enslaved blacks in American history.[1]

The *Tribune* describes an especially grotesque episode of legalized suffering when the heir of a Georgia slaveholder transports 436 enslaved blacks to Savannah for a well-advertised two-day auction. They are housed in horse stalls. The *Tribune* account concludes by describing the sale of a young married black couple. "They were called up," the correspondent writes, "and, as was to be expected, their appearance was the signal for a volley of coarse jokes from the auctioneer, and of ribald remarks from the surrounding crowd." The crowd likely includes all-male white buyers in black hats and black jackets, as in the woodcut of another slave auction. "The newly married pair bore it bravely," the correspondent continues, adding in sarcastic detail, "although one refined gentleman took hold of Frances's lips, and pulled them apart, to see her age."

"The Weeping Time," as this particular mass auction comes to be known, applies as well to an entire era, and tears prompted by the suffering of enslaved blacks—no longer confined to sentimental novels—soon prove the prelude to a sweeping rage. The correspondent leaves *Tribune* readers in no doubt about the moral impact of such scenes: "This sort of thing it is that makes Northern blood boil, and Northern fists clench with a laudable desire to hit somebody."[2]

Sept. 27, 1856.]   THE ILLUSTRATED LONDON NEWS   315

Slave Auction at Richmond, Virginia (1856). *The Illustrated London News*, September 27, 1856.

Frederick's measured, fact-filled prose describing his travels through the South does not make the blood boil. His cool, reasoned accounts, however, win praise in antislavery circles, especially in England. Occasionally, he allows an objective account to carry its own implicit moral commentary. Here in *A Journey through Texas* (1857), for example, he records without comment an exchange between two white Southerners about a runaway slave.

> "If I couldn't break a nigger of running away, I wouldn't have him any how" [said one man.] "I can tell you how you can break a nigger of running away, certain," said another. "There was an old fellow I used to know in Georgia, that always cured his so. If a nigger ran away, when he caught him, he would bind his knee over a log, and fasten him so he couldn't stir; then he'd take a pair of pincers and pull one of his toe-nails out by the roots; and tell him that if he ever run away again, he would pull out two of them, and if he run away again after that, he told them he'd pull out four of them, and so on, doubling each time. He never had to do it more than twice—it always cured them."[3]

This zero-degree writing—as if floating free from an author or style—carries its own stark self-condemnation. While his moral opposition to slavery is clear, he is a gradualist concerned about preparing enslaved blacks for the challenges of freedom and the obligations of citizenship. He writes with the aim of a practical man who values reason over emotion. The death of John cuts him to the bone, however. He increasingly resembles a practical man of action and reason who carries a sorrow within that rarely finds direct expression or relief. He is later subject—not entirely because of incessant overwork—to recurrent breakdowns. It must be said that as architect-in-chief at Central Park he directs a workforce that swells to four thousand men, most Irish, some German, and none of them black.[4]

Marriage for Olmsted—whatever his initial feelings for Mary—is inseparable from the loss of his brother. Romance may be less important than an implied but solemn promise and family cohesion. (Mattie and Hattie are buried on either side of their shared husband.) Meanwhile, as crews in Central Park drain the swamps and chop away at the wild terrain, one intractable dilemma remains: rock.

New York City sits on bedrock. Its trademark skyscrapers soar so high partly because they are pinned to Manhattan schist, the bedrock formed some three hundred million years ago under a miles-deep ocean. Even his new steam-powered tools struggle with rock formations, and Frederick's blasting crews use up more gunpowder, it is said, than was expended at the Battle of Gettysburg.[5] Olmsted's figure runs well over 250 tons. Workers also move nearly three million cubic yards of soil, and plant more than 270,000 trees and shrubs. Frederick frequently opts to leave larger boulders in place—often dark-gray granite outcroppings flecked with silver chips of mica. Elsewhere stone-cutting crews pound away by hand, breaking up chunks to use for paving stones and gravel. Today the half-submerged granite monoliths that remain in place seem to rise from the turf like primordial creatures. Samuel Parsons, who succeeds Vaux as head landscape architect for New York City, writes that "the artistic, and at the same time naturalistic, treatment of rocks in Central Park has no equal, perhaps anywhere."[6]

Struggles with rocks and site preparation offer a distraction, if not relief, from Olmsted's personal grief. Goats roam wild—a nuisance for years as they root up new-planted shrubs—while the lower grounds, as Frederick writes, were "steeped in [the] overflow and mush of pig sties, slaughterhouses and bone boiling works, and the stench was sickening."[7] One gang of workers that Frederick meets on his initial tour of the site is employed in burning underbrush, which both adds to the stench and fills the air with the toxic residue of poison ivy. Olmsted faces challenges wherever he turns, but he also rises to them, as if he had waited his whole life for just this moment. He has tapped into a native genius for melioration.

The challenges and dangers he had faced as a travel writer in some sense provide a training in hardship. Improvisation is an essential skill as he makes his way through the alien South by foot, horse, coach, train, and steamer, with no assurance of finding an inn or even a bed. In South Carolina he improvises a last-minute route to Charleston in what he calls a "little wheel-barrow steamboat"—knowing, after the fate of Andrew Downing, that the boilers aboard even small steamboats can explode. "The cabin was small, dirty, crowded, close, and smoky," he writes amid a prolix economic analysis. "Finding a warm spot in the deck, over the furnace, and to leeward of the chimney, I pillowed myself on my luggage and went to sleep."[8] The improvised pillow also suggests a high tolerance for personal discomfort. Frederick knew about work as an antidote to self-consciousness and personal suffering from reading and discussing the books of Thomas Carlyle. "All true Work is sacred," as Carlyle pontificates in *Past and Present* (1843).[9]

Olmsted describes Carlyle as "the greatest genius in the world."[10] Emerson too as a young man is struck by Carlyle's writing and even visits him in Scotland. After they become close friends, Emerson also arranges the American publication of Carlyle's bizarre parodic novel *Sartor Resartus* (1833–34), full of transcendental musings. Olmsted, despite his enthusiasm for Carlyle, won't let anyone mistake him for "an insane cloud dwelling Transcendentalist," but he also replies fondly to a childhood friend that he hasn't forgotten their "Resartus days."[11] Work for Carlyle is an antidote to the notorious Victorian Doubt, which might be described as an excessive inwardness that questions almost everything, including religious truths. Olmsted, after a brief period of questioning, is mostly untroubled by doubt, and Carlyle simply reinforces his tireless work ethic. In later years he allows himself to wonder, however, if a life of overwork hasn't exacted too high a cost.

∷

Sorrow and suffering, even if he masks them with overwork in his personal life, do not drive Olmsted's more impersonal objections to slavery. The accounts of his travels in the South are designed to make readers think, even calculate. At times they can seem as tediously mathematical as an economics textbook, but then he suddenly redeems his driest passages with vignettes that reveal a pitch-perfect ear for dialogue. It is Charles Dickens in *Sketches by "Boz"* (1836) who popularizes the brief, impressionistic pictures of everyday life that give rise to the new term *vignette*, and Olmsted's originality lies partly in transferring the vignette from fiction to nonfiction. His sketches of everyday life in the South still have the feel of ethnography, in which observations and interviews ultimately support a larger hypothesis: in this instance, that slavery is an unsustainable and ultimately self-annihilating system. Readers unconvinced by his analysis can still appreciate his colorful, if deadpan, shards of local observation. The details, however, always serve a clear but not uncomplicated position. Slavery, as he writes in 1854, is "a fearful cause of degradation of manhood, immorality, superstition and all the evils which in this world attend a disobedience of the laws of Nature and of God."[12] Hard to be clearer. On the other hand, he also holds that abolition is unconstitutional.[13] Slavery must "unravel," as he puts it, but by other means.

The national immersion in suffering deepens as the country edges ever closer to outright civil war. John Brown's prophetic zeal to destroy slavery root and branch ultimately leads to his three-day assault on the US arsenal at Harpers Ferry in October 1859. The assault kills twelve of his followers and concludes with his capture by federal forces under the command, as cosmic irony ordains, of Robert E. Lee. Brown's execution on December 2, 1859, is one more step on the fatal march to war. Thoreau leaps to Brown's defense with an address delivered in Concord two weeks later, against the advice of leading abolitionists who fear his timing is bad, and he does nothing to calm tempers when he publishes the address one year later as "A Plea for Captain John Brown." Olmsted, as former editor of *Putnam's*, might monitor the literary response were he not completely exhausted. Instead, he accepts the board's $500 gift to underwrite a brief leave of absence.

Olmsted lives with daily vexations that even a leave of absence cannot assuage. In fact, it is symptomatic of his increasingly antagonistic relation with the board and with Andrew Green. Just three days before Olmsted's leave begins, the board appoints Green as treasurer and comptroller—at $5,000 per year, twice Olmsted's salary—with an implicit agenda to rein in spending. Even the $500 gift comes with a long string attached: the expectation that he visit European parks. On his so-called leave, Olmsted visits parks and private estates in London, Dublin, Brussels, and Paris. Green also takes full advantage of Olmsted's absence to stage a mini-coup that allows him to assume various obligations of the architect-in-chief, over-seeing staff, firing engineers, and supervising construction. Olmsted loses control over discretionary spending, as Green on one occasion requires an in-person meeting before he will authorize, as Olmsted puts it, "an expen-diture of 12½ cents." Resentful and angry, Olmsted returns to an in-house civil war against what he calls the forces of "Greenism."[14]

Frederick is leading a double life or, on occasion, a triple life. By day, in Central Park, he is directing multiple crews: engineers, stone crushers, landscapers, bridge builders. By night, now married with a young family, he is writing. He publishes *A Journey through Texas* in 1857 and then im-mediately hires journalist Daniel Goodloe to help him revise his collected travel writing. The result, valued by modern historians, is a monumental two-volume book entitled *The Cotton Kingdom* (1861). Olmsted dedicates the book, published in England as well as America, to the British philoso-pher John Stuart Mill, acknowledging Mill's services "in the cause of moral and political freedom." Mill in 1862 returns the transatlantic compliment in a magazine article that opposes slavery, where he openly acknowledges his reliance on "the calm and dispassionate Mr. Olmsted."[15]

###

The national mood is anything but dispassionate. Back in May 1856 Charles Sumner, the senior senator from Massachusetts, delivered a fiery oration against slavery that lasted for five hours over two days. "Even now, while I speak," he insists, "portents hang on all the arches of the horizon, threat-ening to darken the broad land, which already yawns with the mutterings of civil war."[16] It is Sumner who two days later suffers a severe beating by a congressman from South Carolina. Olmsted's dispassionate accounts, whatever their limits, have an unexpected immediate and practical impact. If *Uncle Tom's Cabin* helps ignite the Civil War, as Lincoln suggests, *The Cotton Kingdom* helps to shorten it. Its impact abroad advances the Union cause by helping assure that England with its cotton-hungry textile mills does not intervene, as was long feared, to support the South.

Frederick's exhausting daily work at the park and his grief over the loss of John cannot wholly distract from his financial debts after the failure of Dix Edwards. The machinations of chief engineer Viele and commissioner Green add friction and anxiety. Frederick is not entirely friendless, as his father suggests after John dies, but he is solitary and reserved: one biographer describes his character as "bordering on remoteness."[17] As mere superintendent, he has little power, no future, and immediate threats to deal with, while the promotion to architect-in-chief brings its own new burdens and responsibilities. He is not likely to forget seeing, as he passes through that crowd of angry workers in November 1857, a sign reading "Bread or Blood." The generic slogan, which the wives and widows of Confederate soldiers echo during their hungriest days after the war, is less easy to dismiss when the blood it refers to, as the cost of his job, is Olmsted's blood.

Suffering is inseparable from tragic conflict as the nation sways ever closer to the plunge into a sea of blood. "The dissolution of the Union goes slowly on," Henry Wadsworth Longfellow writes in 1861 from his house in Cambridge that once served as headquarters for George Washington. "Behind it all," he adds, "I hear the low murmur of the slaves, like the chorus in a Greek tragedy, prophesying woe, woe!"[18]

8

***

The Greensward Plan

THE GREENSWARD PLAN—the master plan behind Central Park—can't hope to challenge *Moby-Dick* or the Gettysburg Address in literary value, but it is no less significant as a defining document in the history of America.

There is just one big problem. The Board of Commissioners must vote on whether to accept the late-arriving plan into competition. Thirty-two other submissions have arrived on time. Plan 33, as the Greensward plan is called by the board, has missed the deadline by just a few hours. Charles Elliott has also assured his Democratic colleagues on the board that the author of Plan 33 (supposedly anonymous) is a Republican whom "Democrats could live with."[1] Still, the plan faces an uncertain future even after the six-person Republican majority on the board, as a bloc, votes it back into competition.

The Greensward plan is not simply another everyday blueprint just recorded and forgotten after it has served its disposable purpose. It is more like a visionary multimedia prototype. It combines the new technology of photographs with hand-drawn illustrations and explanatory prose, even including detailed cost estimates for multiple varieties of trees and shrubs. Olmsted and Vaux moreover, in its implementation, continually invoke the democratic principles of a people's park even while they address the challenges of converting an unpromising, barren, swampy terrain criss-crossed with ravines into a cultural treasure enjoyed by the public over multiple generations.[2] Calvert Vaux calls Central Park "the big artwork of the Republic."[3] It is at least worth asking if the Greensward plan—as the foundation of an innovative urban park that has remained a powerful presence both in the United States and worldwide, delighting visitors over the years right up to the present day—should rank among the great creations of the American Renaissance.

###

The Greensward plan might be regarded as a classic transformation narrative. It begins less with a blank canvas than with an actual eyesore. In testimony before the state senate, botanist John Torrey describes the tract considered for Central Park as "bald and unpicturesque."[4] In another master stroke, Vaux recruits an artist renowned for picturesque landscapes, his brother-in-law Jervis McEntee, to create an illustration that depicts the bald tract before its transformation. McEntee obliges, depicting a rock-strewn and hardscrabble terrain that offers nothing to draw the eye, no contrast, no texture, no variety, just empty sky and shapeless land. It is nature devoid of aesthetic charm: a visual analog of Henry James's famous list of things absent from American life. The treeless void constitutes surely the least picturesque work in the entire and extensive McEntee canon, but it works perfectly within the Greensward plan among the carefully crafted

Jervis McEntee, *View in Central Park, New York City* (1858). New-York Historical Society (N-YHS), gift of Mrs. Lyda M. Nelson, reproduced with permission.

before-and-after illustrations. Olmsted's calm and dispassionate prose, honed on his Southern travels, adds persuasive verbal reinforcement to the visual images, which ultimately add up to an implicit nonfiction narrative of a change. It does not promise the sudden, magical change of fairy tales but rather creates a plan for the incremental work of melioration designed, in stages, to transform an urban wasteland into a vast urban picturesque landscape unlike anything before it in the brief history of America.

The Greensward plan reclaims 778 acres of wildly subprime Manhattan real estate, soon expanded in 1859 four blocks north to the park's present 843 acres. The picturesque natural scenery will change as the newly planted trees mature, and the clientele will also change, as the first mostly upper-class parkgoers in their carriages are joined, beginning in the 1880s, by an influx of immigrants and working-class families. Slowly, in pace with social changes, the park begins to keep its republican promise of providing for the common good. It also proves a model for public parks across America and the world. Everything begins, however, with the Greensward plan and its multimedia transformational design.

The Greensward plan does not impose its vision on the land but rather works through accommodation and compromise with the existing terrain. The bluffs, swamps, and boulders already establish certain practical limits. The Board of Commissioners, in setting the rules for its open competition, adds particular requirements. The rectangular Old Reservoir, still in daily service, can't be moved. All plans must include a parade ground, a formal flower garden, playgrounds, a site for concerts, a prominent fountain, an observation tower, and a venue for ice skating. Not quite as an afterthought, it specifies no less than one institution of "cultural uplift or practical knowledge."[5] The most worrisome requirement: four roads to cross the park. Here Olmsted and Vaux respond to the constraints with a brilliant innovation and propose to sink the four transverse roadways eight feet below ground level. The solution not only prevents dividing the park into quadrants. It conceals the crosstown traffic from parkgoers, while artfully placed bridges, plantings, and walkways both enhance the concealment and create the impression of an uninterrupted, flowing terrain. The effect is more than visual. Today you can walk forty blocks in Central Park without a pause, except perhaps on Sundays if you encounter an unfordable stream of bicyclists and runners.

Greensward as a title is a master stroke of marketing or grantsmanship. It evokes a rural, romantic, slightly archaic aura recalling the novels of Sir Walter Scott, where it appears some twenty-seven times, if my online search is accurate. Olmsted twice uses the term in *Walks and Talks* referring to an open stretch of grass-covered turf or meadow.[6] Central Park, however, is hardly a meadow. It deliberately mixes *meadows* with *woodland* and *parkland*. Parkland refers to a mix of trees and grassy vegetation, while a landscape that features bluffs, ponds, boulders, cinder paths, and a large new reservoir hardly resembles a greensward. The term serves less to describe the landscape, however, than to provide an attractive and memorable name, distinguishing it from its nameless rivals. Titles, as Olmsted knows as a writer and editor, are crucial in their slightly mysterious appeal, while providing a catchy shorthand reference. The Greensward plan comes with a ready-made brand name.

The Board of Commissioners, with thirty-three plans to discuss, takes six weeks to announce its decision on April 28, 1858. The Greensward plan wins top prize, including a $2,000 cash award. Olmsted can now pay down a few debts even after splitting the award with Vaux. Most important, several weeks later the board offers Olmsted the position of architect-in-chief.

Not everyone is happy. Olmsted's new salary of $2,500 falls short of the board's original provision, but at least it offers a small raise over his salary as superintendent. His title, which ignores his total lack of training in architecture, long remains a source of irritation to Vaux, who is hired at $5 per hour as a mere "assistant." It takes another half year before Vaux is elevated to the role of consulting architect, but he perseveres. As he later tells Olmsted, it was "of course somewhat difficult to countenance the idea of an established architect serving as clerk for six months to a new man who chose to call himself or be called architect, but I chose to risk it trusting to the truth working itself out."[7] Trust and perseverance can entail their own risk-taking. An effective response to global climate change will need more than a few people like Vaux. It is Viele, however, whose irritation openly explodes.

Politics, it turns out, may matter as much as good design when it comes to winning a competition. Olmsted is a Republican whom Democrats can live with, and Viele is a Democrat whom Republicans can live without. The Greensward plan prevails thanks to first-place votes from all six Republican commissioners. The one first-place Democratic vote, significantly, is cast by Andrew Green, who in his later role as penny-pinching comptroller replaces Viele as Olmsted's villain-in-chief.

The party-line vote suggests that Vaux is canny, as usual, in choosing a Republican as his partner to create a design for the park, but he also later admits that, by himself, he was "wholly incompetent to take it up."[8] The two semi-vagabonds, Olmsted and Vaux, together accomplish what neither alone could do, combining strengths and minimizing weaknesses.

The Greensward plan is the product of unqualified partners who barely know one another, but who both can sense that the moment is right. In seizing the opportunity, they also open space for additional collaborations. Thousands of immigrant workers and artisans combine to transform the scrubby wasteland into a gorgeous park, and the workforce that maintains the park today—from gardeners and arborists to mechanics and painters—shows how large urban parks can provide steady jobs for individuals and economic benefits for the community. Its intangible or concealed benefits, from public health to civic pride, are not all a direct product of the Greensward plan, but they ultimately depend on the unlikely partnership between a vagabond London architect and a New England travel writer who, but for Vaux, would have been a farmer. The Greensward plan not only brings Central Park to life but also offers a model for the inventive and unpredictable collaborations we need today.

The epic sweep of the Greensward plan is reflected in the size of the gigantic accompanying diagram, eleven feet long by three feet wide. Epic size, however, is at odds with the minimalism of the plan's two underlying basic principles: *follow the terrain* and *balance the irregularities*. Olmsted and Vaux follow the terrain even in creating the new mix of meadows, woodland, and parkland, but they also create new terrain by flooding low-lying areas to create the Pond and the Lake. Vaux in *Villas and Cottages* describes how picturesque settings harmonize the natural terrain with architectural elements in a "well-balanced irregularity."[9] The irregularities of the Lake and the Ramble offset or balance the symmetries of the Old Reservoir and the Mall, as an incredible fifty-eight miles of paths meander through the landscape like rivulets in patterns that lie somewhere between geometry and the fractal asymmetries of the natural world.

A bird's-eye view of the lower park around 1860 shows the Mall (or Promenade) at the center, pointing like an upturned hairbrush toward the rectangular Old Reservoir, in contrast to the flowing paths, irregular pools, and varied terrain. Carriages enter the park from the south on a slightly curved drive leading directly to the oblique angled Mall. The overall effect illustrates how much variety Olmsted and Vaux manage to introduce by adhering to those two basic principles. A third underlying or unseen principle is also at work, however, visible mostly in comparisons that juxtapose images of the park in 1860 with images of the park today. Olmsted and Vaux insist the design must always—its paramount rule—*anticipate the effects of time*.

Principle three might be called the forty-year rule. "When Mr. Vaux and I first put our heads together in study of the design for the Central

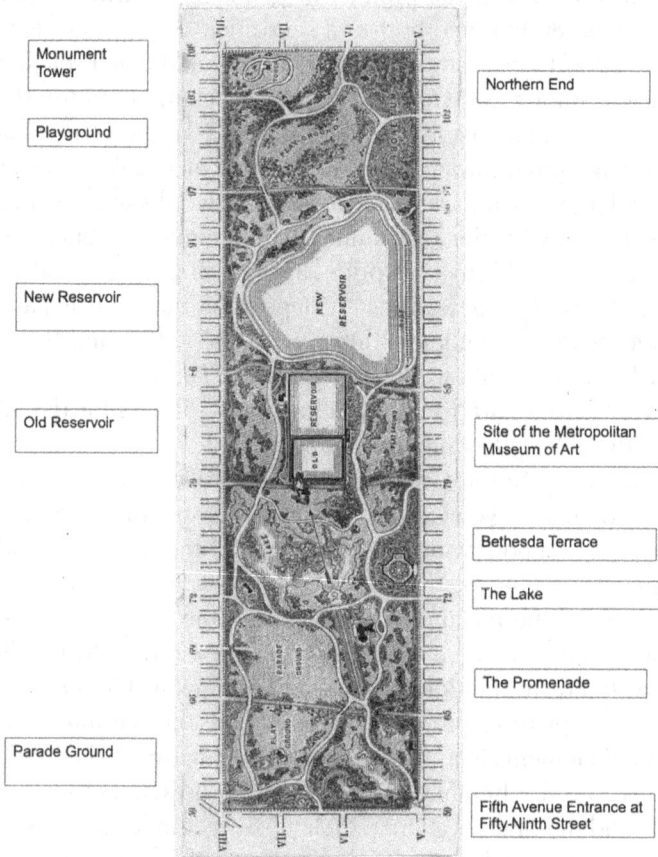

Map from Greensward Presentation, board no. 2 (1858). Department of Parks and Recreation Drawings Collection, NYC Municipal Archives.

Park," Olmsted writes, "we agreed to treat nothing as of essential consequence, except with reference to results which might be looked for, at nearest, forty years ahead."[10] Forty years does more than acknowledge the inevitable passage of time. Olmsted's earlier visit to another famous English park prompts a passage in *Walks and Talks* significant enough that he later repeats it verbatim in a letter to the board. The park, he writes, constitutes "a picture so great that Nature shall be employed upon it for generations."[11] Central Park orchestrates the effects of time like an inaudible musical score that swells over forty years. Olmsted and Vaux, however, are not looking at a specific four-decade end date, when the park will reach its

View of Central Park in 1860. Library of Congress.

climax of perfection: the long-awaited conclusion. Olmsted specifies forty years "at nearest." The elms that flank the Mall in symmetrical double rows have life expectancies of four hundred years.

The transformations basic to the Greensward plan, far from mere visual tricks, change swamps into meadows, ditches into gentle dells, and buried creeks into flowing ponds and lakes. Even muck excavated from the swamps is recycled as topsoil. Although the entire park is technically artificial, meaning human-made, the reshaped landscape and newly created water features are material changes that hardly constitute, as one distinguished scholar writes, instances of "illusion."[12] There is nothing illusory about trees and shrubs, or about bridges, arches, and rustic structures. Thousands of benches in four styles are spread across the park today, while many original features of the terrain—bluffs, crags, and promontories—are retained or reconfigured within an altered setting. Olmsted himself describes the "extraordinary and gravely difficult duty" he faced in preparing to transform "a broken, rocky, sterile, and intractable body of land."[13] Frederic B. Perkins, brother of Olmsted's runaway bride-to-be, in 1868 publishes an account of Central Park describing the space that Olmsted transformed. "In its undrained hollows," he writes, "stood stagnant pools, or cold swamps and bogs." In sum: "It was a miserable realm of barrenness, stench, filth, poverty, lawlessness, and crime."[14]

The Ramble offers a typical instance of the artful transformations by which the Greensward plan creates, in effect, a new nature. Clarence Cook in his 1869 account recalls the original site as "an unsightly mass of particularly barren rock, on which even mosses and lichens refused to grow; the soil thinly spread between the ledges was too poor to support any but the toughest and least graceful shrubs, while along its centre there ran a bit of soggy marsh." Then come the beautiful changes. "To-day," Cook continues, "no rock is seen but such as is needed for picturesque variety; the rest is covered with earth, or overlaid so thick with honeysuckle, wild grape, trumpet-creeper, or wisteria, that its presence is not suspected by the passer-by." He concludes his description with a local twist to the nineteenth-century myth of the American Adam, which depicts humankind as reborn free from Old World sin, innocent and unfallen, the chosen possessors of a God-given New World paradise. "A more unpromising locality," writes Cook in his unauthorized version of Genesis, "was never given to any Adam to make an Eden of."[15]

The forty-year rule, identifying time or duration as the third principle underlying the Greensward plan, is never far from Cook's descriptions. He praises Olmsted and Vaux for their artful use of plantings to soften the starkness of the bare boulders so prominent in the Ramble, affirming that "every year's growth of trees and shrubbery makes the nature more, and the art less, so that, in time, it will only be the nature that will attract attention, and the art will be lost sight of." He greatly admires a feature of the Ramble popular then but lost today: a half-hidden cave, with its romantic hint of hermits or secluded lovers. "Here a man may sit for hours," Cook writes, "and hear no sound but the chirp and twitter of the birds, the rustle of the light breeze overhead, or the far-off murmur of the town."[16] The pleasure of solitary concealment amid urban crowds is basic to nineteenth-century accounts of the flâneur, while birdsong and cool breezes are the opposite of artifice or illusion. They are instead the predictable and entirely natural outcome of planting 270,000 trees and shrubs. The Greensward plan and Central Park show what is possible when urban environments embrace contact with the natural world.

⁝⁝⁝

The principle of duration built into the Greensward plan has a special resonance as Olmsted and Vaux imagine Central Park in relation to a future New York City. They accurately foresee a time when Manhattan will flatten its natural terrain and smooth its irregularities into roadbeds and buildable lots. Central Park, in this future-perfect view, will have preserved what the city, in its inevitable growth and development, has destroyed and forgotten. "Then," as Olmsted writes about Central Park, "the priceless value of the present picturesque outlines of the ground will be more distinctly perceived." He continues with something like a manifesto applicable to parks everywhere: "It therefore seems desirable to interfere with its easy, undulating outlines, and picturesque, rocky scenery as little as possible, and, on the other hand, to endeavor rapidly, and by every legitimate means, to increase and judiciously develop these particularly individual and characteristic sources of landscape effects."[17] How successful are Olmsted and Vaux in following their own principles? "Well," as *Tribune* editor Horace Greeley remarks after inspecting the newly opened park, "they have let it alone a good deal more than I thought they would!"[18] Olmsted, writing to Vaux in 1887, agrees: "The great merit of all the works you and I have done, is that in them the larger opportunities of the topography have not been wasted in aiming at ordinary suburban gardening, cottage gardening effects. We have let it alone more than most gardeners can." Then, in a reflective afterthought, he adds with a self-critical pause: "But . . . hardly enough."[19]

The Greensward plan embodies one final and crucial concept that only the material transformations of the landscape can realize. Olmsted on his early visit to Birkenhead Park feels an almost spiritual connection to the land, as if he feels reunited in a bond of deep connection. "Gradually and silently," as he reflects in *Walks and Talks*, "the charm comes over us; the beauty has entered our souls; we know not exactly when or how, but going away we remember it with a tender, subdued, filial-like joy."[20] I share such feelings as I walk around the reservoir. The calm I feel on my walks often carries over, mixed with other thoughts, as, say, I watch a squirrel racing over the bare branches building a winter nest. Central Park offers a connection with the natural world that includes a peaceful sense of openness. Olmsted believed that parks could meliorate human behavior, and even the dogs seem oddly meliorated. Runners checking their smart watches are more concerned with intervals—personal-best times are also a form of melioration—but, as unspoken comrades, we all join the flow of visitors returning, like grown children, to a place that we may dimly suspect we left once a long, long time ago.

9

▮▮▮

The Wiping Out of Seneca Village

CENTRAL PARK, amid Olmsted's sorrow over the death of John and amid the national crisis of war, is entangled in its own particular history of irreparable loss, not unrelated to the losses that minority communities today experience in the destruction from unprecedented floods and perhaps distantly linked to the larger devastation implicit in global climate change. Species are now going extinct at an unprecedented rate. "It is estimated," writes Elizabeth Kolbert in *The Sixth Extinction* (2014), "that one-third of all reef-building corals, a third of all freshwater mollusks, a third of sharks and rays, a quarter of all mammals, a fifth of all reptiles, and a sixth of all birds are headed toward oblivion."[1] Up to one million animal and plant species are threatened, many within decades, but we can't see or admit it.[2] Central Park too involves losses that remain almost unknown until historians and archaeologists begin piecing together lost fragments of a middle-class and mostly African American community known as Seneca Village. Seneca Village is swallowed up during the creation of Central Park, wiped out as if it had never existed, while the former residents scatter and even its memory disappears.

Disappearances are not all equal. They range in origin from political murders and ethnic cleansing to psychic repression, as unwanted reminders are erased from thought. Some disappearances are, at least in part, reversible. The wolves returning to Yellowstone Park and the coral reefs recovering off Palau show that biological systems can possess a regenerative resilience. Seneca Village, however, never recovers. Its irreversible loss demonstrates the legal power of majority cultures to dispossess powerless minorities, justified by invoking the public good. The headstones covering six hundred acres at Arlington National Cemetery speak of personal sacrifice for the public good not borne equally across all social groups. Central Park in its magnificent achievement is inseparable from its losses, including the deaths of five workers, but until recently the disappearance of Seneca Village has been largely unacknowledged and unhonored.

The Commissioners of Estimate and Assessment face a daunting task with little guidance in calculating payments. There are 561 known landowners among the 1,600 people residing within park boundaries, and many landowners remain unknown or unlocated. The commission, as Roy Rosenzweig and Elizabeth Blackmar explain, needs to decide on "the value of each of the 7,520 lots and the 300 or more structures on the site of Central Park and to develop a system for assessing the surrounding property owners who would help pay for this land." The commission delivers its report in October 1855, when New Yorkers learn that taxpayers will be billed $5 million for the land, while landowners adjacent to the park are assessed $1.7 million based on projected increases in property values.[3] Few people like taxes and special assessments, while the commissioners receive seven volumes of complaints from landowners protesting low assessments. The civic willingness to raise substantial funds to underwrite an extensive, major new urban park offers a challenge to economies facing the perils of climate change. The challenge extends to close attention to the human and natural costs.

▟▛▙

Seneca Village, according to census figures for 1855, had a population of 225, two-thirds African American, including a number of landowners, a status rare then for black people. Property worth at least $250 is a requirement for black voters in local elections, and Seneca Village in 1855 lists 10 African Americans on the voting rolls—or 10 percent of blacks on the voting rolls citywide.[4] The community is home to whites as well, often Irish renters, and includes some fifty homes, three churches, and one school. One other set of figures is important to recover, however, in understanding the disappearance of Seneca Village. In its first twenty years, starting in 1858 with the opening of the Pond and quickly followed by the Lake and the Ramble, Central Park saw carriages outnumber pedestrians. Gatekeepers kept meticulous records. "For every four million New Yorkers who arrived at the park in carriages and on horseback in the 1860s," Rosenzweig and Blackmar report, "another three million or so came on foot." It was the upper classes alone who could afford carriages, the latest luxury vehicle, as the working poor could barely feed themselves, let alone afford horses.

Central Park is neither the product of an illegal land grab nor the creation of a consciously racist conspiracy. The inequalities and the dislocations, however, no matter how fairly black landowners are compensated, fall heaviest on African Americans and on immigrants unable to resist the bureaucratic machinery of a white-run power structure. Slowly but surely, the "eminent gentlemen" (as the *Tribune* describes them) who make up the Commission of Estimate and Assessment, white all and all wealthy, combine in the name of the state to erase Seneca Village from the face of the earth.

▖▖▖

As park supervisor hired to prepare the site, Frederick Law Olmsted certainly knows about Seneca Village. He also knows how legislative power is used to oppress. The Fugitive Slave Law (1850) means that New York, even as a free state, cannot exclude bounty hunters looking for escaped slaves, whom they forcibly return to plantation owners, at whose hands the escapees face certain reprisal, including torture or death. Olmsted despises the Fugitive Slave Law. He "would take in a fugitive slave & shoot a man that was likely to get him," he writes as a young man.[5] Bravado is not Olmsted's style. He tends more toward quiet arrogance and unshakable self-confidence, in which his moral opposition to slavery never wavers. The emancipation of enslaved blacks in the South, however, also raises constitutional questions that in his thirties lead him to adopt a go-slow position on emancipation regarded as "gradualist."

"The conviction that freed slaves would be unprepared to instantly assume the duties and responsibilities of free citizens," as biographer Witold Rybczynski writes, "was central to Olmsted's gradualism."[6] While gradualism seems a tepid response, for Olmsted it reflects his developing views on freedom. While he supports freedom for enslaved blacks, he distinguishes between freedom and liberation. Freedom is a civic condition; liberation is a sudden act. The practice of freedom, he believes, requires more than a sudden act of liberation, although even this view is open to revision.

In *The Cotton Kingdom* (1861) he describes slavery as a form of outright tyranny. The only valid democratic response to tyranny is to overthrow it. "It is said that the South can never be subjugated," he writes in 1861, when the outcome of the war is still largely in doubt: "It must be, or we must."[7]

Meanwhile, after the state legislature votes in 1853 to fund a new park, the work of the eminent gentlemen estimating damage and assessing payments grinds on. It takes two years to buy out and eliminate Seneca Village. Olmsted oversees the crews charged with its material eradication.

Frederick Douglass, an escaped slave and renowned orator, travels in 1859 from New York to Detroit for a secret meeting with John Brown. He ultimately declines Brown's invitation to join him in the raid at Harpers Ferry, but Douglass later describes Brown's execution in 1859 as the "thunder clap" that awakens the nation from its moral slumber and rouses it to war. Olmsted hears the thunder rumbling, but he is also locked in struggles with the board and with its cost-cutting comptroller, Andrew Green. By fall 1859, Frederick is burning past the point of exhaustion, in bed for an entire week with fevers. He says he is hardly able to raise his head.[8] His exhaustion is why the board, alarmed, grants him a six-week leave beginning in late September, adding a $500 subsidy for a tour of overseas parks. Olmsted's ten-week antidote for illness and exhaustion includes visiting six private estates, two royal gardens, and nine public parks.[9] He does not return until mid-December. Moral slumber is a less immediate problem than getting enough sleep, although he dimly senses that behind the scenes his former ally Green is plotting to replace him. Chronic exhaustion and insomnia accompany a lifetime of somatic symptoms that he treats, no thanks to Carlyle, with habitual overwork.

▪▪▪

Seneca Village lies concealed beneath the turf of Central Park until the 1990s, when historians and archaeologists start piecing together the shards. Historians Roy Rosenzweig and Elizabeth Blackmar are instrumental in sparking this recovery with their brief but seminal account in *The Park and the People* (1992). Their account centers on Andrew Williams, a black resident who in 1825 buys three lots in Seneca Village. Williams lives next door to the African Methodist Episcopal Zion church, which also vanishes without a trace once demolition begins. The city pays Williams $2,335 for his land, which includes a modest two-story house: a substantial sum, but less than Williams claims he has been offered.[10] It takes him thirty years to resolve his dispute with the city.

Excavations at the Seneca Village site directed by archaeologists Diana diZerega Wall and Nan Rothschild have uncovered artifacts that reflect people living in a stable lower-middle-class community, while park historian Sara Cedar Miller has recently added substantially to our knowledge of specific residents.[11] A decorative blue teapot, for example, suggests values and desires incompatible with hardscrabble living. Melioration is not an objective limited to the carriage class.

The origin of the name Seneca Village has long remained a mystery. I propose that it refers to the drive among free blacks for education and moral self-improvement. Olmsted in *The Cotton Kingdom* observes, for example, that "the coloured population voluntarily sustain several churches, schools, and mutual assistance and improvement societies." He then cites a newspaper account describing an episode close to Washington in which some twenty-four "genteel coloured men" are suspected of meeting to plan "mischief," meaning most likely sedition. The men, as it turns out, belong to a benevolent society dedicated to relieving the sick. The few books found in their possession include the Bible and, to my surprise, *Seneca's Morals*.[12]

Seneca's Morals, a translation of essays by the Roman philosopher Seneca the Younger, is reprinted multiple times since its first appearance in 1678, and its Stoic reflections on ethical issues often coincide with a Christian outlook. Seneca Village, I strongly suspect, takes its name from the religious and moral high seriousness with which freed African Americans pursue a self-education denied to enslaved blacks. The well-documented religious and educational values embraced in the small community of Seneca Village were visible in its *three* churches, the centers of social life, and *Seneca's Morals* is a fund of moral insight relevant to the local congregations. "There's no condition of life that excludes a wise man from discharging his duty," the translation informs its readers. "If his fortune be good, he tempers it; if bad, he masters it."[13]

The wiping out of Seneca Village is an episode in an ongoing American saga that regularly pits the power of the state against minority groups, including the poor and the powerless.[14] The legal seizure of property owned by the black residents of Seneca Village did at least provide the displaced landowners with compensation, and with an opportunity to dispute values that seemed unfair. The black residents, however, stood no chance against the legal machinery of the nation, state, and city, which already denied them full rights. Sara Cedar Miller in her brilliantly researched study indicates that, among the figures in Seneca Village who received compensation, porter Simon Green was awarded $1,280 for two lots on Eighty-Fifth Street, which he originally bought for $700; James Hinson, a cooper, was awarded $1,080 for two lots on Eighty-Fourth Street, which he originally bought for $325.[15] Miller is well aware of the chicanery, but nonetheless offers this conclusion about the awards granted by the Commission of Estimates and Assessment: "With the exception of some landowners who paid inflated prices in 1852, most people made a profit, and a handsome one at that."[16]

The disruption of a settled community, however, cannot be measured entirely in profits. William G. Wilson, for example, emerges from oblivion as a pillar of his community. His house, which he shares with his wife and eight children, has a rare stone foundation. A property owner and voting citizen, Wilson also serves as sexton at the adjacent All Angels' Church: a brick structure with a predominantly African American congregation. All Angels' Church too is swept away in 1859 as Olmsted's crews clear the ground for Central Park. Two other Seneca Village churches, likely built of wood, disappear under the hammer of eminent domain. One exception: All Angels' Church is moved brick by brick a few blocks west, outside the park. Significantly, the congregation scatters. Only a single resident of Seneca Village joins All Angels' in its new location. Final eviction orders come on October 1, 1857, and Seneca Village simply disappears.

###

The disappearance of Seneca Village is hardly unique in the history of urban renewal, and visitors certainly enjoy Central Park today without knowing its fate, although historical markers, online histories, and archaeological work mean that the disappearance is not total. The park carries traces of its invisible past, along with other less human disappearances. The Old Reservoir has disappeared, for example, now vanished beneath the Great Lawn with its playing fields and rock concerts. Central Park is more than the sum of its lawns, trees, and boulders. It is bundled up in untold stories.

The magic of Central Park is not exempt from sentiment that borders at times on kitsch. Currier & Ives in 1868 depicts a proto-Disney nighttime scene in which the full moon illuminates upper-crust couples gliding across the park in their horse-drawn sleighs as skaters glide across the frozen lake, offering a romantic backdrop including Bow Bridge in the distance like a winter rainbow. It is too perfect. It is almost pretty enough to make you

Currier & Ives, *Central Park in Winter* (1868–1894). Metropolitan Museum of Art, bequest of Adele S. Colgate, 1962.

forget that they are gliding over a massive artificial park where the law of eminent domain wiped out a small mixed-race community of people who could not afford a sleigh ride. The loss of an entire neighborhood—225 people, almost two-thirds African American—differs from the dispossession of scattered landowners, often white, absent or simply unlocated. It is a familiar story. A 2007 report from the Institute for Justice focusing on the Housing Act of 1949 finds that over the next twenty-five years more than 2,500 projects using the power of eminent domain displace 1 million people, two-thirds of them African American.[17] The magic of Central Park is achieved only at the cost of significant if often unseen human loss.

▪▪▪

Seneca Village is not the only serious loss. It is a warm summer day in 1860, August 6 to be exact, and Olmsted is driving his open horse-drawn carriage on a rare outing with Mary and their newborn son, just two months old. Maybe Frederick falls asleep at the reins, or he just loses control. The mare bolts. A carriage wheel slams into a lamppost, flinging Olmsted against a boulder. "Things turned black," he writes later, "and I thought

I was dying."[18] Passersby carry him on a makeshift stretcher to a nearby house. Mary and the baby, astoundingly, are unhurt. Bruised and lacerated, Olmsted is not all right. Fragments of bone stick out of his leg—three splintering fractures of the thigh that extend through the knee.[19] The doctor, on seeing the horribly mangled leg, wants to amputate immediately. On reflection, as Olmsted later reports, the doctor explained that "if he cut off my leg I would not live through the night; if he did not, I might live a week."[20] The odds that Olmsted will survive, as he's told, are no more than one in a hundred.

No major New York City newspaper carries an account of the accident, which suggests that Olmsted's near celebrity status comes only well after his work on Central Park. Not the *New-York Daily Times*, not the *New York Herald*, not the *Brooklyn Daily Eagle*, not the *Brooklyn Evening Star* has a word to say. This is especially surprising as there are other references to Olmsted in August 1860, mostly ads and notices for *A Journey in the Back Country*. The only source to mention the accident, as far as I know, is the *National Anti-Slavery Standard*. It is printed in New York City, and the edition for August 11 runs a brief notice in the personal column.[21] Then, on August 25, a second notice appears: "Frederick Law Olmsted, Architect-in-Chief of the Central Park, who has been laid up some weeks with a broken leg, caused by being accidentally thrown from his carriage, is rapidly recovering, and expects soon to resume his active duties."[22] It is worth asking why the only paper to report on his near death and notable recovery is adamantly opposed to slavery.

Olmsted is a hard man to kill. There is no amputation; he survives the first week, and soon his staff make their reports at his bedside. Later, wrapped in bandages from hip to toe, he conducts regular inspections carried around the park in a litter chair, while Andrew Green again seizes the opportunity to consolidate power behind the scenes.[23] Two months later, still splinted and hobbling on crutches, Olmsted in October 1860 supervises police protection for Prince Albert's official visit to the park. Albert, husband of Queen Victoria and a well-known reformer, plants a ceremonial English oak, while Green—the board-designated host—plants an American elm. No one thinks to introduce Olmsted to the prince. Finally someone points to Olmstead. The prince, as Frederick writes to his father, "turned & bowed to me several times until he caught my attention."[24] Like a well-bred gentleman, Olmsted returns the bow.

He is still bandaged hip to toe, unable to sit in a chair or turn over in bed, when Mary leaves on a visit to Boston. She thus misses both the royal nod and the park luncheon that Olmsted arranges with sculptor Emma Stebbins and actress Charlotte Cushman. Stebbins has been selected to create a sculpture to place atop the unbuilt fountain that will anchor the unnamed lakeside terrace. She is the first woman in New York City commissioned to create a public artwork, and Cushman will be her model for the fountain-topping, larger-than-life bronze angel. Stebbins and Cushman are lovers, notorious for daring to wear men's hats, but they set aside their bowlers for respectable dark gowns in a photograph that includes the signs of their professions: the sculptor's uncovered right hand and the actor's book. The fountain and its crowning sculpture today constitute a much-admired visual icon. Despite his injuries, Olmsted seems somewhat

Emma Stebbins and Charlotte Cushman (c. 1870). Harvard Theatre Collection, Houghton Library, Harvard University.

bemused at the prospect of lunching with two such well-known and some-what scandalous artists.

"Wife being away," he writes to his father, "I fall among the Bohemians."[25]

Three months after his luncheon with the Bohemians and the prince's royal bow, Olmsted submits his letter of resignation to the board. Soon he too disappears.

10

▞▞▞

An Escape from Buildings

ESCAPE HOLDS AN unappreciated significance for Frederick Olmsted. His wandering and restlessness may embody implicit personal acts of break-out or flight. He escapes in effect from his father's dry-goods store. He escapes from life as a surveyor, a seaman, a gentleman farmer, a travel writer, an editor, and even a first-time landscape architect. Central Park, however, transforms random personal getaways into a founding principle. The purpose of an urban park, Olmsted later states explicitly, is to provide an "escape from buildings."[1]

Escape implies a release from confinement, and confinement is what buildings come to signify for Olmsted. Buildings of course can also signify shelter and safety, but even as a child Olmsted preferred wandering out-doors. His later equation between buildings and confinement, however, is not strictly a personal idiosyncrasy. New York City in 1860 is a booming national hub of commerce, finance, and industry, the largest city in the United States with a population rapidly swollen to more than 800,000. Immigrants and the working poor spend large chunks of time indoors, in factories, sweatshops, and windowless tenements, while the upper classes keep carriages and "take the air." Buildings in their height and density are what begin to define the visual profile of New York City—in contrast to spread-out, low-slung colonial towns such as Williamsburg, Virginia. The cost of freedom for many immigrants recently arrived in New York City is a life increasingly pent up in buildings.

Buildings as a fact of city life also function for Olmsted as metaphors for a life of confinement. Thoreau in rural Concord sees the mass of his work-consumed neighbors confined by lives of "quiet desperation." Olmsted by summer 1859 sees his workforce swell to 3,600—a brigadier general commands almost as many—and the work is all-consuming. Free time is a fantasy, especially after his marriage to Mary in June 1859. He also keeps working on his magnum opus, *The Cotton Kingdom*. Olmsted's promotion to architect-in-chief means that he oversees an engineering corps, independent cartmen, stonecutters, blasting gangs, road gangs, paving gangs, derrick gangs, rock gangs, and site grading gangs, not to mention gangs of landscape gardeners and even thirty blacksmiths. Each gang has a foreman, whose daily production Olmsted monitors. Time itself has become a new and ingenious medium of confinement. Job seekers pursue him in the evening at home. "Dear Father," he begins a letter in September 1859. "I have been besieged by fevers for a week and this is the first I have done but lie on the bed or sofa." He adds, nearing despair: "I feel just thoroughly worn-out, used up, fatigued beyond recovery."[2]

Overwork is as much an Olmsted signature as his trademark cane, and it is likely overwork (causing the carriage accident) that hobbled him for the rest of his days. Work is his own personal confinement, as later he and his firms carry out commissions at forty college campuses, fifty residential communities, more than one hundred public parks, and two hundred private estates.[3] The stamina he spends on Central Park alone is extraordinary. The board meanwhile turns up the heat, appointing Andrew Green as comptroller to monitor expenses in response to politicians and newspapers grousing about costs. Green, the lone Democrat who votes in favor of the Greensward plan, is a bachelor who once dined regularly with Frederick and Mary. No more. *Park Wars* may be an exaggeration, but Frederick has good reason to feel not only harassed about costs but also betrayed: Green, it becomes clear, wants his position as architect-in-chief. Worn down, a new father with three adopted young children, writing at night, by day commanding a small brigade of gangs, foremen, and immigrant workers, Olmsted is still in debt and fighting to protect the Greensward plan from cost-cutters and revisionists. Bouts of insomnia, depression, jaundice, paralysis, vertigo, rheumatism, tinnitus, and typhus remain lifelong maladies. He is, as one biographer puts it, "emotionally taut."[4] Once, learning that an executive committee has rejected his proposal, he bursts into tears.

Buildings are a convenient metaphor for less visible forms of confinement such as overwork, and New York City has no lack of buildings. A large urban park thus offers more than trees and grassy meadows. It offers a metaphoric release from the gospel of work. It offers a freedom from politics and harassment. A walk in the park is a metaphor for ease, contentment, and whatever we just like to do.

###

Escape from buildings, whatever its metaphoric resonance, remains a key literal concept for Olmsted. Escape, however, while it implies a prior confinement, functions for Olmsted not like a jailbreak but like a temporary respite. With New York City increasingly defined less by geography than by its buildings, Central Park offers urban dwellers a temporary reprieve from multiple confinements. His opposition to buildings cannot overrule the board's initial requirements for a few specific structures. The required armory (or arsenal) already existed on site, but in his compromises with the board Olmsted never backs down from his fundamental belief that the purpose of an urban park is to provide a liberating escape from buildings. If he must accept the requirements of the board, he does not have to agree. "The reservoirs and the museum are not a part of the Park proper," as he insists, using his own defiant, principled arithmetic: "they are deductions from it."[5]

Olmsted is onto something important in the association between an urban park and freedom from confinement. The famed film director Frederick Wiseman in his almost three-hour documentary *Central Park* (1990) focuses on people in motion: an uninhibited free play embodied as walking, running, climbing, skating, boating, picnicking, or just sunning on a hillside in slow motion.[6] Known for exposing typically American institutions from schools to hospitals as systems of confinement, Wiseman portrays Central Park as inherently anti-institutional: defined less by place or by policies than by unconfined movement. A squabble over permits to sell T-shirts simply emphasizes a general absence of regulations. The park for Wiseman is not a source of postcard-like static images but rather a venue for the celebration of bodies in motion, spontaneous and kinetic, like the fluid dancers and skaters that his camera lovingly follows. Central Park is where people are relieved of institutional baggage and social controls. Even the park police keep a low profile, visible only in Wiseman's film as they book a drug dealer. The glimpse indirectly identifies the park as a protected space where unconfinement rarely slips into crime or anarchy, as Olmsted intended in his invention of "keepers." Occasional shots of the city let Wiseman suggest that this joyful, unconfined free play occurs as if in an enchanted realm just beyond the reach of buildings.

■■■

The differences between Olmsted and Vaux are significant and center on their opposing views of parks and buildings. Vaux is clear when he states that nature in Central Park is primary and architecture secondary. Unlike Olmstead, however, he does not see buildings as a deduction from the park. As an architect trained to design buildings, he doesn't seek to escape them but rather—this is the crucial point—to integrate them into the landscape, much as the artist's studio that he designs for Jervis McEntee nestles into its natural surroundings. For Vaux, buildings and landscape go together: they form a conceptual unit. Thus, in addition to the necessary bridges and arches, Vaux at Central Park contributes various modest picturesque structures such as a dairy and scattered rustic huts. A so-called Conservatory proposed in the Greensward plan—a glass mansion for plants—never gets built, although it endows the small pond adjacent to the site (now a seasonal home to ducks and model boats) with the extremely puzzling name Conservatory Water. Olmsted later insists that the term architect is misused and should also apply to landscape. "Architecture is not rightly to be limited to works of buildings," he asserts.[7] Short of linguistic reform, however, Olmsted's only recourse is to squeeze buildings into parks through a conceptual loophole. "Building can be brought within the business of the Park proper *only*," as he paradoxically reaffirms his basic principle, "as it will aid escape from buildings."[8]

Escape is inherently bidirectional. You escape *from* confinement and *to* freedom. The escape *from* buildings matters to Olmsted as the indispensable first step of an escape *into* nature. Nature in Central Park, of course, does not resemble a wilderness or a backwoods tangle of underbrush. The Ramble may embody a dim dreamlike *memory* of wilderness, but it is a simulated wilderness. The Mall or Promenade even offers a deliberate and geometrical tree-lined exception to the fluid paths and picturesque irregularities that dominate elsewhere in the park. The appeal of Central Park lies in the pleasures of nature domesticated and managed for human enjoyment: a welcome temporary alternative not to crowds but to indoor confinement. "There are indeed few gayer or better attended promenades in Europe," Olmsted writes in 1861, "it having been not at all unusual during the last year for 2,000 carriages and 10,000 persons on foot to enter the gates of a fine autumn afternoon."[9]

Working-class New Yorkers do not make up a substantial percentage of visitors to Central Park until the 1880s, when they launch a successful campaign for concerts in the park on Sundays, their one day of rest.[10] Baseball, soaring in popularity after the Civil War, comes rather slowly to the park: the Greensward plan proposes a cricket field. From sport to concerts to picnics, however, the underlying idea holds firm. The park offers an escape *from* buildings and *into* nature shaped as an alternative to its urban surroundings and their human cost.

The human cost of urban life as signified by buildings might be defined as the opposite of well-being. Sick building syndrome, for example, is "a major occupational hazard" in the age of global climate change. Headache, dizziness, nausea, dry cough, itching skin, fatigue, allergies, flu-like symptoms, asthma attacks, personality changes, and irritation of the eye, nose, or throat—the list goes on—count among its familiar symptoms.[11] Indoor air pollution is inescapable when its sources include adhesives, carpeting, upholstery, manufactured wood, copy machines, and pesticides, to name just a few. Common cleaning fluids can produce both chronic and acute health effects, with homes often no safer than workplaces.[12] The trees and shrubs that Olmsted and Vaux add to the landscape are more than decorative, in both eliminating disease-breeding swamps and providing filters that clean and cool the air. Outside buildings and inside the park, we enter a temporary space that is comparatively free from indoor toxins, although not wholly free today from the harmful effects of global climate change.

Water too is more than a decorative landscape feature at Central Park. Human bodies are roughly 60 percent water, and we die quickly without it. People are drawn to ponds, lakes, rivers, streams, and oceans as if instinctively. It surprised me to learn, however, that the hordes who arrive when the lower park first opens in December 1858 are ice skaters. Water converted to ice draws some three hundred skaters on the very first Sunday, but by the second Sunday the number swells to ten thousand. On Christmas Day maybe twice that number.[13] The Greensward plan inherited two nonnegotiable bodies of water: the existing rectangular Old Reservoir and the projected oval New Reservoir. The 106-acre New Reservoir now offers stunning views of the Manhattan skyline from the surrounding path, although in Olmsted's day there was no path and the elevated banks *blocked* views of the water. It thus it failed to qualify as what the Greensward plan calls "a landscape attraction."[14] Today it attracts an endless stream of runners, walkers, and photo-seeking tourists, advancing the goal of the Greensward plan to create "the most agreeable contrast to the confinement, bustle, and monotonous street-division of the city."[15]

The two reservoirs, beyond their contributions to human well-being, offer a revealing snapshot of Central Park as an organic creation that changes across time as needs change. The Old Reservoir, built in 1842, entirely disappears. It had stored drinking water, which New York City receives today piped in from a network of nineteen reservoirs and three lakes. No longer needed, the Old Reservoir during the 1930s is filled in and covered over to create the Great Lawn. The New Reservoir—an engineering marvel completed in 1862—is decommissioned in 1993 and renamed in honor of Jacqueline Kennedy Onassis. Its former maintenance path at first serves as an informal running circuit, but a multimillion-dollar endowment later upgrades it and names it the Stephanie and Fred Shuman Running Track. "If you've ever been to this track at the end of the day," Fred Shuman tells a reporter, evoking another image of unconfinement, "you can't believe you're in New York. It smells like the ocean."[16]

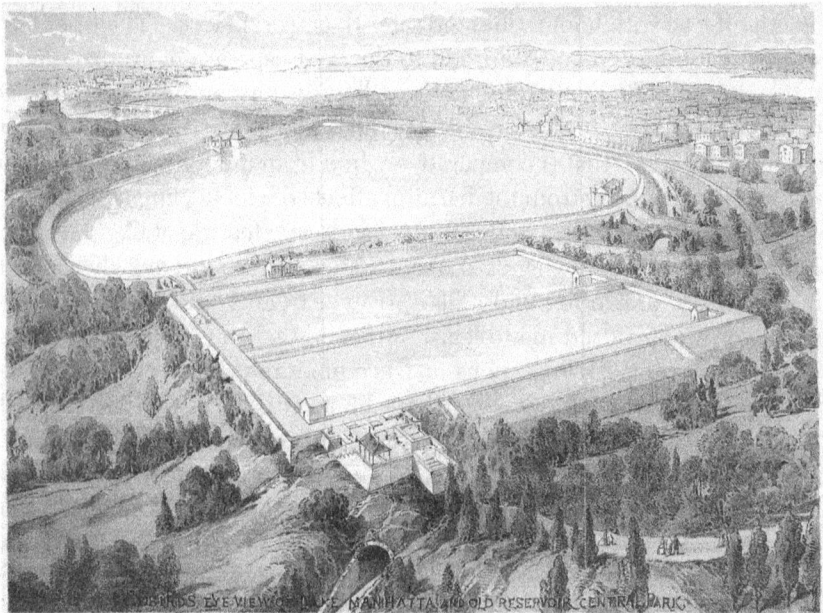

Birds Eye View of Lake Manhatta and Old Reservoir, Central Park (1871). New York Public Library Digital Collections.

Central Park possesses an epic quality reflected in the herculean task of transforming a semi-wasteland into a cherished, enduring 843-acre urban refuge. The transformation narrative, however, is less epic (with an inherent closure, as in the hero's return home) than novelistic, reflecting a fundamentally open-ended temporal structure in which characters come and go, change and disappear, and in which the action seems indefinitely extendable, as apparent endings turn into the provocation for sequels and spinoffs. Successive generations reconfigure the zoo; for example, once it receives permanent quarters in 1871 and instantly—like ice skating—ranks among the park's most popular features. (Who knows if future generations will find the confinement of nonhuman animals unacceptable.) In 1927 August Heckscher donates the first equipped playground. A good idea, but as in a Dickens novel new characters keep popping up. Robert Moses, the czar-like figure appointed Commissioner of the New York City Parks Department in 1934, adds some twenty playgrounds, including baseball fields on the Great Lawn.[17] Central Park is in perpetual motion, as full of changing storylines as a soap opera.

How does a swamp become a lake? There is a story for that. The Lake and the Pond exist only because thousands of immigrant workers drain the wetlands, excavate bogs, move soil, and break up huge rock formations using picks, shovels, baskets, and horse-drawn carts. A natural lake or pond will die if deprived of a supporting ecology, and the Greensward plan creates a mini-ecology in its call for planting some 150,000 trees and 150,000 shrubs—far more than the 270,000 that actually take root. The parkland trees and shrubs, of course, need people to plant them, and Olmstead's instructions require unseen, time-consuming care: "The roots must be opened and spread out with the fingers upon a bed of carefully worked, fine mold. Fine mold must then be worked and pressed in among the roots near the trunk with the fingers, until there are no cavities left to be filled."[18] Hidden pipes and sluices control the water levels at the Lake and at the Pond, which can be lowered in winter for skaters and raised again in the springtime for boaters. Workers move some three million cubic yards of dirt, topsoil, and rock. Samuel Parsons, who later works closely with Vaux, offers a different measure that coincides, not surprisingly, with Olmsted's own published estimate: "if all the carts that were filled with earth in the construction of Central Park were strung out in one line, it would reach 30,000 miles, or one and one-fourth times around the earth."[19]

View in Central Park, New York (c. 1859). New York Public Library Digital Collections.

A time-lapse film of Central Park would expose and emphasize the perpetual motion that mostly passes unnoticed amid the apparently solidity of a stable and rock-solid landscape. "We determined," writes Vaux, "that the Ramble should be the picture that people would come to see."[20] This picture, however fixed it may appear in nineteenth-century illustrations, is anything but static, and today the Ramble immerses visitors in tree-choked corkscrew paths, ravines, and boulders that deny any possibility of aesthetic distance or vistas. We are less spectators than active participants: immersed *within* the moving picture. Some may even stumble and wrench a knee. Central Park continues to change beyond its original vision in the likeness of an English pastoral painting or picturesque landscape. The changes do not always constitute what Olmsted would regard as clear improvements, since perpetual motion also creates openings for entropy and decline. Twenty years after resigning his post at Central Park and leaving New York City, Frederick is dismayed by what he sees on a return visit, complaining that in his absence the beloved park has taken on "a slovenly and neglected aspect."[21]

■■■

Central Park at moments exposes its likeness to a living time capsule. An iron chunk is fished out of the reservoir almost by accident. Later, recognized as part of the original protective fencing, it provides a pattern for the facsimile that now rims the Stephanie and Fred Schulman Running Track. Large-scale repair and renewal, however, are not as simple as fishing up a section of cast-iron fence or resurfacing a running track. The climate system today includes multiple linked, irreversible tipping points that defy exact calculation, from the collapse of Greenland's ice cap to the melting of the carbon-rich Siberian permafrost with its slumbering pathogens. An 843-acre park does not offer a model for how coastal cities might avoid being swallowed up by rising sea levels or a strategy for figuring out how to prevent the skies from raining down fire and chaos. It can, however, serve as an important source of encouragement and hope as we get on with the work of repair that we need to undertake. "A man used to go and sit in Central Park wearing elaborate golden robes," as writer Doris Lessing explains in an interview. "He never once opened his mouth, he just sat. He'd appear at lunchtime. People appeared from everywhere, because he was obviously a holy man, and this went on for months. They just sat around him in reverent silence. Eventually he got fed up with it and left."[22]

███

Central Park, funded just two years after the publication of *Moby-Dick*, is epic in its ambition but most like a novel in its embrace of what theorist Mikhail Bakhtin calls "unfinished contemporary time."[23] Time and change are exactly what Olmsted and Vaux build into the organic structure of Central Park in their forty-year rule, and the concealed genius of Central Park may lie in its capacity to adapt over time. What can seem like purely natural, organic powers of change and self-renewal—as the trees in spring suddenly fill the park with greenery and teams of workers tend the grounds—also offer a hopeful promise of *melioration*, in Emerson's useful term. Unfinished contemporary time enfolds implicit provisions for change in concert with the natural world if we can act wisely, with a concern for future generations and without relying on or waiting around for saviors. The pressures of contemporary unfinished time now encompass the dangers of a new and not-entirely-fictional sense of an ending. The Doomsday Clock updated each year by the *Bulletin of the Atomic Scientists* in 2025 moves the time to eighty-nine seconds before midnight.[24] It is in effect an alarm clock, but it sometimes feels like the remote device set to trigger a planetary time bomb. Olmsted and Vaux as if running out of time keep working tirelessly to complete their new urban park, staggering in its scale and demands, but it is the nation in fact that ultimately runs out of time.

On April 12, 1861, after years of smoldering conflict, the South Carolina militia attacks the Union garrison at Fort Sumter in Charleston Harbor and plunges the nation into an irreversible, blood-soaked, doomsday-like civil war.

11

###

Sideways Time Travel

"MY PICTURE IS all alive," Olmsted rejoices as Central Park takes shape, adding: "Its very essence is life, human & vegetable."[1] Central Park as a living organism has a temporal as well as a spatial existence. It embodies a paradox that Olmsted recognizes and rejoices in: a landscape painting that pulses with life.

Its pictorial or visual qualities lend Central Park a stable appearance, but the stability is deceptive. Breezes rustle through the leaves, seasons change, visitors leave at dusk and return at dawn. Birds dart among the branches, and unseen microbes burrow deep in the soil. The park sways to the biology of time, malleable, changing, alive—host to complex, symbiotic relationships among humans, plants, animals, insects, and microscopic organisms so dizzying in their flux and flow that it may prove helpful to drop a few anchors of old-school linear chronology:

1852   *Walks and Talks of an American Farmer* is published
1853   New York State approves funding for Central Park
1857   Olmsted is appointed park superintendent; John dies
1858   The Greensward plan wins the open competition for design
1859   Olmsted, now architect-in-chief, marries John's widow, Mary
1861   Civil War begins; *The Cotton Kingdom* appears

It is an eventful decade, considering that Olmsted manages to complete three journeys through the prewar South, to publish four books, to win the design competition for a massive new park, to get married, to adopt three children, and to supervise the creation of the colossal, first major public works project in America. Timebound, he spends fewer than four years at Central Park before leaving to accept two managerial positions that have nothing whatever to do with landscape.

A straightforward linear chronology—assigning fixed, verifiable dates to major events—is not the only measure of time. Last month I walked almost daily around the reservoir, but I couldn't tell you on exactly which days, or what the weather was like on Thursday. These previous walks do not exist as memories, exactly—since I can't remember them—but more like experiences absorbed into some other dimension of time and mind. Central Park obviously possesses a fixed address. It could probably receive its own mail there. Its existence in time, however, seems to possess a strange duck/rabbit duality, both linear and nonlinear. Time flows through Central Park with an uncanny sideways motion, not always straight like an arrow from before to after, but rather with a tendency to zigzag, overlap, eddy, and interpenetrate. The crowds flowing through the park like time travelers with untold stories are as basic to its nature as rocks, trees, and boulders.

***

The changes rippling through Central Park, as material as the growth rings of a tree, support Olmsted's assertion that its essence is life, both "human & vegetable." The people are thus not extraneous to the park but rather inseparable from its status as a living organism. The idea of Central Park as a living, organic creation that *includes* human life tends to slip away whenever I try to imagine the many millions of visitors stretching back to 1858 who have walked its paths or enjoyed romantic carriage rides, adding unknowable loops of experience that interrupt any straightforward linear history. Suppose you parachute back into 1896. Who is the gentleman in the photograph of Bethesda Terrace who adjusts his hat, or perhaps tips it in greeting, while he walks toward the famous fountain? Nostalgia is beside the point. The four-year economic panic beginning in 1893 has just begun to recede. Why has he come? Who are his companions? Are they gay, straight, or exactly who they seem? Are they the graduates of segregated schools? Ageing former residents of Seneca Village seem nowhere in sight, while an interest in eros draws my eye to the well-dressed couple under a parasol. Time travel doesn't guarantee that you'll like what you find, but it

*Bethesda Fountain,
Central Park* (1896).
New York Public
Library Digital
Collections.

highlights how far Central Park envelops much more than the motionless sum of its 843 linear acres.

Time is less like the linear path of an arrow than like a parabolic arc or a deep borderless pool. It is life filled with endless unheard voices. "I visit Central Park now almost every day, sitting, or slowly rambling, or riding around," writes Walt Whitman in May 1879.[2] Easter Sunday 1967 sees ten thousand people gather in Central Park for a Whitmanesque "Be-In." It is the Summer of Love, and the gathering in Central Park follows an even larger event two months earlier in San Francisco, flower-power capital of the Psychedelic Sixties. "Actually it's a hip Easter parade," says playwright Sally Ordway, evoking a distinctive New York tradition as she strolls past two young men with balloons attached to their neckties. "Look at those hats," she continues, "look at those helmets, look at those bananas that people are wearing." A spectacle it is, as bananas and balloons vie with carnation petals, paper stars, and tiny mirrors pasted on foreheads. "I'm wearing my wife's cerise tights," says copywriter Bruce Maddox as the celebrants press onward to the Sheep Meadow, once a military parade ground, "because it's the one thing I could get in a bright color."

The *New York Times* reports that the helmeted, fruit-clad, colorful visitors are chanting "L-O-V-E."[3] The chant carries a political subtext. US military advisers stationed in Vietnam during the 1950s begin to increase significantly in number by 1961, and in 1965 they are joined by active combat units. *Being*—the goal or action of a Be-In—is more than an esoteric theme for philosophers and theologians. The Be-In as a form of antiwar protest implicitly opposes *being* with *nonbeing*: a colorful counterculture alternative to the grotesque daily body counts and kill ratios out of Vietnam. US forces suffer some ten thousand casualties by mid-1967. Olmsted and Vaux include a military parade ground, but it's unlikely they imagine it repurposed one day as a grassy space for picnics and antiwar demonstrations. The Easter Sunday celebration is about much more than balloons. *Being* has an everyday face. As James Fouratt, one of the organizers, explains: "We wanted it to be a celebration of being alive, of having that experience in the park." "People in New York," he adds, "don't look at each other, don't see each other, don't talk to each other."[4]

The *Times* describes Fouratt's dawn-to-dusk jamboree as "noisy, swarming, chaotic and utterly surrealistic." Not pointless, though. Central Park quietly affirms the First Amendment freedom of Americans to gather peacefully and to chant L-O-V-E while wearing a banana. *Being*—a consciousness of existence over time—is worth a celebration. I hear the voice of Frederick Olmsted as an old man as he corresponds with the woman he had silently loved back in New Haven when he was a drifting special student at Yale. She congratulates him on his lifetime of distinguished achievements. He responds dryly, as if recalling the biblical prototype of self-betrayal, Esau: "I have been selling being for doing."[5]

⁝⁝⁝

The Sheep Meadow just one month after it hosts the Easter Be-In welcomes a very different gathering. It is a cold, damp April morning, and serious protestors arrive to attend a mass rally advertised under the heading "End the War in Viet Nam."[6] Martin Luther King Jr., after a round of speeches, leads a march to the headquarters of the United Nations. The path from Central Park to the UN is more than an arbitrary route. Central Park as a people-centered space seems almost umbilically connected to the institution created to address conflicts among nations. The UN, however, is restricted by its own bureaucratic structure of dues, vetoes, and committees. The Sheep Meadow is where people assemble not only outside buildings but also outside bureaucracies. Thousands of gay men and women march in protest from Greenwich Village to the Sheep Meadow on June 28, 1970, marking the first anniversary of the notorious police raid on the Stonewall Inn. The march is credited as a key moment of change in the movement for gay rights. Martin Robinson, in charge of political affairs for the Gay Activities Alliance, notes the significance: "We've never had a demonstration like this."[7] Central Park is not the arbitrary endpoint but a destination: a symbol of freedom and change.

New Yorkers love parades—an online guide for visitors lists forty-seven annually—and Central Park as a destination for marchers and as a backdrop for spectators is a parade magnet. The famous Easter Parade stops just short of Central Park on its northward trajectory up Fifth Avenue, as if even the fanciest bonnets can't compete with the daffodils and azaleas—or perhaps the park is a secret rendezvous once the parade stops at Fifty-Seventh Street. In 1880, nine thousand Freemasons march up Fifth Avenue as prelude to a cornerstone-laying ceremony in the park. Fifty thousand cheering spectators attend a second ceremony in 1881 to dedicate an obelisk erected on the site.[8] Thirty-two horses in sixteen teams transport the two-hundred-ton granite pillar from the East River. The colonial politics are now forgotten, but Cleopatra's Needle (as it is mistakenly called today) has arrived because the US consul general at Cairo has secured it in exchange for US neutrality as France and Britain maneuver to control Egypt. The Trojan Horse seems almost clean-handed by comparison, but Central Park in its openness to the flow of unfinished contemporary time can't exclude violence.

Cruxy O'Connor in 1922 is ambushed and shot four times by gunmen from the Irish Republican Army, just outside Central Park at Eighty-Fourth Street and Fifth Avenue. Engaged in a struggle against British military occupation, the IRA suspects that O'Connor is a turncoat. The ambush happens in front of horrified spectators, some no doubt just exiting the park, and also contains elements of slapstick.[9] One gunman, after throwing away his pistol, misses the getaway car and is left facing a horde of eyewitnesses. He escapes, amazingly, and Cruxy O'Connor survives. Central Park too survives the era of contract killings and submachine guns, but its winding pastoral paths nonetheless turn sinister in the 1970s as violence moves inside the park and muggers roam freely.

On an evening run in Central Park on April 19, 1989, Trisha Meili is brutally assaulted and raped. The police find her in a shallow ravine, gagged, tied, and covered in mud. She lies in a coma for twelve days, so close to death that a priest administers last rites. Meili survives, although with lifelong disabilities, later publishing a memoir and dedicating her life to helping survivors of sexual assault.

The ensuing legal prosecution of the so-called Central Park Five clearly demonstrates how racism and its poisons are impossible to exclude from Central Park. Two weeks after the assault on Trisha Meili the police arrest five teenage males, all either black or Latino. They maintain their innocence, but they are convicted and jailed amid a larger national frenzy over race and crime. Thirteen years later, in 2002, an imprisoned murderer confesses to the awful assault. DNA evidence confirms his guilt, and the city withdraws all charges against the young men. In turn they sue New York City for malicious prosecution, racial discrimination, and emotional distress, reaching a settlement after more than ten years for $41 million. A documentary film by Ken Burns, Sarah Burns, and David McMahon, *The Central Park Five* (2012), enlists the awful episode among their explorations of American experience. There is, however, one additional turn of the screw. Yusef Salaam, one of the Central Park Five, in July 2023 wins the Democratic primary for a seat on the New York City Council, an improbable feat for a political novice, where he soon wins election.[10] "Those who have been close to the pain," he puts it, "should have a seat at the table."[11]

Central Park is unable to exclude the toxic residue that leaks in from the surrounding culture, but the wonder is that even its recent conflicts remain relatively peaceful. Another drama plays out in the Ramble in 2020 when a white woman in her forties, walking her dog, calls the police to accuse an older black man, a bird watcher, of threatening her after he asks that she restrain the dog. Central Park cannot escape its location as a middle ground where different life histories collide. "What she did was tap into a deep vein of racial bias," says Christian Cooper, the man whom she falsely accused.[12] Central Park cannot eliminate racism, alas, but in a city that regularly witnesses subway stabbings, mass shootings, and domestic violence it offers a space where occasional eruptions of bias, racism, and crime seem almost a sacrilege.

⊞

Central Park is a poor choice if you want to remain invisible. People-watching is a favorite pastime of parkgoers. I like watching the joggers as they pass me on the running track, mute characters in my own private narrative, each spandex-clad storyteller with a tale I'll never get to hear as they whip past me in all shapes, sizes, and ages. I enter at East Ninetieth Street, greeted across the water by the twin towers of the El

Dorado, a soaring Art Deco building akin in its double towers to the San Remo further south. Both buildings share the same architect, so the resemblance is not surprising, but I prefer the El Dorado because I like to imagine its famous residents—Groucho Marx, Marilyn Monroe, Bono, Pinchas Zukerman—standing at their windows, waving as I start my morning circuit. I feel as if my chest expands as I gaze across the open stretch of water. Maybe Olmsted is right about openness as a hidden principle behind the escape from buildings. The reservoir offers a visual image of *breathing room*. The skaters on fancy rollerblades seem more companionable than the joggers, not least because rollerblading is an urban art form, dance on wheels, with high-speed twists, twirls, and breathtaking jumps. Rollerbladers are performers in outrageous costumes, like acrobats. There is even a Central Park Dance Skaters Association.

Art, too, especially painting and music, lends its texture to the folds or layers in the extended fabric of time that constitutes Central Park. Zorach Gorfinkel, a Lithuanian immigrant, and California-born Marguerite Thompson are American painters who in 1911 meet in Paris, at exactly the right moment to catch the origins of modern art. Marguerite is the more daring artist. "I just couldn't understand," he writes later, "why such a nice girl would paint such wild pictures." Returning to America, they marry on Christmas Eve 1912, both take Zorach as their married surname, and both exhibit work in the legendary 1913 Armory Show. (Zorach Gorfinkel is now William Zorach, and their Greenwich Village apartment becomes a haunt for modern artists.) Their mutual affection extends to a love of nature, urban and rural, as William implies in his painting *Spring in Central Park*. The painting features two idealized lovers who resemble a modern, unfallen Adam and Eve. Central Park is an ideal scene of innocence and love, and the biblical scene is a Zorach family favorite. "We made our little hall into a garden of Eden with a life-sized Adam and Eve," William writes of their apartment, although the depiction also includes "a red and white snake draped around the trunk of a decorative tree."[13]

Spring in Central Park too evokes an almost archetypal link with the Garden of Eden, minus a serpent. The lovers bow their heads in a communion of spirits tenderly as nature enfolds them in a nurturing embrace. Trees bend forward to create a canopy, and flowers bloom on cue. Bow Bridge is another favorite setting for couples who flow through the park each spring: a romantic backdrop for photographs that capture, in its erotic dimension, what James Fouratt calls a celebration of *being*.

People-watching is often at its zenith when the people are also watching animals. A zoo, required but not included in the Greensward plan,

William Zorach, *Spring in Central Park* (1914). Image copyright © The Metropolitan Museum of Art. Image source: Art Resource, NY.

is authorized by the state legislature in 1861, initially called the Central Park Menagerie. It soon contains in its shifting locations a bear cub, an elephant, and a South American peccary. General George Custer contributes a rattlesnake, while the Barnum & Bailey Circus donates a bull bison, a species hunted close to extinction. The bison, named Black Diamond, serves as a model for the famous "buffalo nickel" minted from 1913 to 1938, although after his star turn he is sold to a slaughterhouse in 1915 and reduced to buffalo steaks.

Animals belong within the flow of time that washes through Central Park, some even honored with statues, such as the bronze sled dog Balto. Animal behavior, however, at times seems in conflict with the values of a picturesque retreat. "A park," as Clarence Cook writes in 1869, perhaps quoting Olmsted, "is a place of rest and recreation for mind and body" where "nature soothes and tranquillizes the mind." He particularly objects to a gift that the board—which holds ultimate authority—accepts: a large bronze sculpture entitled *The Tigress and Her Cubs*. The "tranquil, rural beauty of the Park," Cook asserts, should avoid any reference to "carnage and rapine" in its purpose "to lift the spirit of man to a higher region." A tigress carrying a dead peacock to feed her hungry cubs is, in his view, "far better suited to a zoo."[14] Presto. The offending sculpture moves in 1934 to the courtyard of the Central Park Zoo, which gains a permanent seven-acre

Auguste Caine, *The Tigress and Her Cubs* (1867). Albert Fitch Bellows, in Clarence C. Cook, *A Description of the New York Central Park* (1869; repr., New York: New York University Press, 2017).

quarters in 1871. Managed today by the Wildlife Conservation Society, the zoo in its changes demonstrates the layering that makes Central Park a living palimpsest on which succeeding generations inscribe their own overlapping hopes, fears, and sometimes conflicting desires.

░░░

The current construction of the eleven-acre Harlem Meer Center in the far northeast corner of the park belongs to a determined effort to extend an openness and welcome to minorities. The $160 million project replaces the former Lasker Pool and Rink, a dangerous eyesore from the mid-1960s, and is meant to serve the largely black and Latino communities nearby. Yusef Salaam, now representing Harlem from his hard-earned seat on the city council, recalls swimming in the Lasker Pool with his sneakers on because the bottom was littered with broken glass.[15] The city contributed an initial $60 million for the project, with the Central Park Conservancy and affiliated donors contributing the balance. Some might see the Harlem Meer Center as an overdue act of civic recompense or atonement for the losses at Seneca Village. Time in its eddies occasionally offers an opportunity, rightly seized, to correct wrongs, to redress injustice, and (as Cook writes) to lift the spirit such that the people's park may truly serve *all* the people.

The daffodils in Central Park are blossoming now earlier than ever in mid-February. Short-term temperature fluctuations are normal. England, amid an extended period called the Little Ice Age, records its coldest winter in 1684 and two years later records its warmest winter. Climate scientists, however, also see in the Central Park daffodils yet another unwelcome sign that the planet is heating up.[16] Olmsted and Vaux, after the first flush of triumph following selection of the Greensward plan, have other anxieties as they wake up each morning to the immense work of creating an unprecedented urban park from a rock-strewn tangle of semi-wilderness—amid a fragile republic that has now fallen into all-out civil war.

12

A People's Park

THE EMBERS FROM the Los Angeles fires of 2025 are still smoldering as fears grow about the approaching heavy rains, which may extinguish the embers but also trigger catastrophic mudslides and toxic runoff, poisoning the groundwater. The fires enfold rich and poor alike. Almost two centuries earlier the French diplomat and political philosopher Alexis de Tocqueville visits the United States, soon afterward publishing his classic work, *Democracy in America* (1835/1840). Tocqueville, as he is known, is not impressed by democracy as a political system, fearing it will lead to a tyranny of the majority, but rather by Americans as a people. Olmsted reads *Democracy in America* in preparing to write a book that he never finishes, and he cannot have missed the powerful first sentence. Among the striking innovations he notices in the young republic, "none struck my eye more vividly," Tocqueville writes, "than the equality of conditions."[1]

An equality of "conditions"—meaning social rank—might well impress an aristocrat born with the name and title Alexis Charles Henri Clérel, comte de Tocqueville. He is well aware that equality does not apply to Native Americans and to African Americans. He foresees the "frightful principle" of slavery as the "most dreadful of all the evils that threaten the future of the United States."[2] Indeed, his visit coincides with Nat Turner's Rebellion in 1831. Still, despite his fears for its future, what strikes Tocqueville so vividly in America is a social mobility and personal independence that put its white citizens on an equal footing. Vaux too, arriving twenty years later from London, expresses amazement at the fluid social scene, and what dismays him most are the renegade Americans who aspire to European manners and distinctions, selling their liberties (as he invokes the familiar biblical image) "for a mess of pottage on the old aristocratic plan."[3]

Olmsted in effect reverses the journeys of Tocqueville and Vaux when he and John in 1850 take their walking tour through England. A Connecticut Yankee, Olmsted shares enough pride in American democracy that he is shocked on his visit to Birkenhead Park. What strikes him there so vividly is the diversity of social classes enjoying their so-called People's Garden. Earlier European parks are most often royal gifts, but the citizens of Liverpool finance their new park almost entirely through public subscription. The resulting mix of social classes at the park inspires Olmsted, as a traveler from a newly democratic land, with awe and chagrin. As he observes of the parkgoers from the fabled land of monarchs, "There were some who were attended by servants, and sent at once for their carriages, but a large proportion were of the common ranks," including "the wives of very humble labourers." He adds, "The poorest British peasant is as free to enjoy it in all its parts as the British queen."[4]

Birkenhead Park is less egalitarian than Olmsted sees at age twenty-eight. The Grand Entrance with its classical columns sixty feet tall clearly reflects imperial ambitions and social divisions. Carriages enter through the wide center arch, while the wives of humble laborers and pedestrians use smaller flanking arches. Equality of conditions and democratic values, however, remain primary in their thinking as Olmsted and Vaux work on the Greensward plan. Instead of a grand entrance, the Greensward plan imagines four principal points of entry along its southern border, where most visitors arrive. The low *gates*, as they are called, are dedicated to "the people"—defined not by social class, wealth, or rank but by their work: Artisans, Artists, Merchants, and Scholars.[5]

On Sundays, rain, shine, or subzero cold, I walk across the park from East Sixty-Eighth Street to West Eighty-Fifth for breakfast with my daughter, who teaches at Barnard College. Our academic talk reminds me that it seemed an odd choice to dedicate one of the four original gates to scholars. Then I remember that Emerson's famous address "The American Scholar" does not refer to professors or academic life but, as he puts it, to "Man Thinking."[6] The designation *Scholar*, as the park commission clarifies in 1882, includes "the Poet, the Divine, the Statesman, the Lawyer, the Author, the Editor, the Teacher, the Physician, [and] the man of Science."[7] This inclusiveness or equality of conditions, however, does not settle a controversy over a grand entrance. The gate debate, reflecting a split over architectural style almost as deep as civil war, pits native egalitarian mini-malists against advocates of monarchial grandeur. But, first, an interlude.

###

Olmsted's vision of Central Park as pulsing with human life takes shape in family gatherings far more extensive than my Sunday morning break-fasts. It is a principle that he embraces throughout his career. Parks are not just elegant landscapes but places meant to draw people in. My route across the park and back on Sundays is irrational: taxis, a luxury, would be quicker and drier. Twice a downpour has caught me mid-park and thor-oughly soaked me. Families too arrive at the park, defying the weather and every reasonable disincentive, in order to enjoy group picnics, ballgames, and reunions. Olmsted in a lecture on Brooklyn's Prospect Park describes both its magnetic power to draw people in and its power to cross lines of age, rank, and class. He counts "near twenty thousand children with their parents, Sunday-school teachers, or other guides and friends, who spent the best part of a day under the trees and on the turf." "In all my life," he concludes, "I have never seen such joyous collections of people. I have, in fact, more than once observed tears of gratitude in the eyes of poor women, as they watched their children thus enjoying themselves."[8]

People are the missing link in a strictly landscape-focused analysis of parks. A liberation from buildings has as its counterpart a democratic social inclusion. The aesthetics of landscape design matters to Olmsted, but it matters mostly as the design serves to attract people across classes and conditions. The debate about a formal entrance to Central Park, which can seem simply a squabble over style, thus raises basic political and social issues on which Olmsted and Vaux, despite their differences, share very strong opinions. Here ends the interlude.

###

What is a park? The question, which seems to expect an objective answer, might be reframed from a subjective, political, and social perspective to ask, in defiance of grammar, who is a park *for*? In practice, Central Park is slow in fulfilling its democratic promise, and its first two decades are dominated by horse-drawn carriages and upper-class display. Although by 1865 the park hosts well over seven million visits each year, more than half the visitors arrive in carriages, while rules banning group picnics actively discourage lower-class immigrant visitors, at least until the 1880s.[9] Olmsted, nonetheless, is clear about where he stands on questions of democratic inclusiveness. The "one great purpose" of Central Park, he writes as its earliest features open to the public in 1858, is "to supply to the hundreds of thousands of tired workers, who have no opportunity to spend their summers in the country, a specimen of God's handiwork that shall be to them, inexpensively, what a month or two in the White Mountains or the Adirondacks is, at great cost, to those in easier circumstances."[10]

Absences are sometimes as significant as what is present. What the Greensward plan doesn't contain amid its balanced irregularities and flowing paths is a Birkenhead-like Grand Entrance. In April 1864, however, the board considers this absence a serious mistake, and it directs Andrew Green to begin planning for the construction of not just one but four impressive gates. The board also chooses its designer, Richard Morris Hunt, the Paris-trained brother-in-law of a sitting board member. Hunt's French-inspired imperial designs, put on public display, clearly violate the democratic spirit of the Greensward plan, but Olmsted has left New York for California. In his absence it is the indispensable Calvert Vaux who springs into action as the bulldog-like defender of Central Park, its expression of democratic inclusiveness, and what he explicitly calls *the republican art idea*.

Vaux launches a multifront campaign against the four new gates, in the press, at dinner parties, and in the halls of power.[11] The proposed gates, he argues in a May 1865 letter to the *Evening Post*, reflect an "imperial style": an autocratic, aristocratic tradition in which ordinary people, humiliated, "hang around" waiting while the emperor tends to his "clients, courtiers,

Richard Morris Hunt,
Central Park Gate
(c. 1860s). Library of
Congress Prints and
Photographs Division.

subordinates, [and] lackeys." Vaux drives home his anti-imperial rant by borrowing a satirical figure from earlier British theater, the Grand Panjandrum. This pompously despotic character serves as almost a metaphor of absolutism and vain display. "But when the New Yorker enters his park," Vaux continues with a republican flourish, "the great panjandrum enters exactly at the same moment and in the same suit of clothes."[12]

Art critic and ally Clarence Cook follows up the Vaux assault with a supportive column in the *New-York Daily Tribune*.[13] "Mr. Hunt seems to have a grudge against Nature," he begins. Cook's column, unsigned as usual, goes on to praise Vaux's letter in the *Evening Post* and explains that the park is "founded on the purest and most elevated democratic ideas"—with "no fixed classes"—unlike Hunt's Eurocentric, expensive, and grandiose plan: "the barren spawn of French Imperialism." Its "Americanism" is what Cook calls the "most striking feature" of Central Park. He thus lambastes the proposed gates as not only "ugly and unsuitable" but also, crucially, "as un-American as it would be possible to make them." Cook, friendly with Vaux, adds repeated insults in his lengthy takedown, but his most shrewdly original claim is that the Hunt gates express "no freedom, no play." Playful is exactly what Hunt's designs are not. They express instead only a despotic, aristocratic ambition. "We don't like to be reminded of the existence of such riff-raff as the French Emperor," Cook adds, firing a gratuitous salvo at the Confederate-sympathizing Napoleon III, "when we are in our Park."

"Unscrew the locks from the doors!" Walt Whitman exclaims in his ecstatic praise of American openness. "Unscrew the doors themselves from their jambs!"[14] Vaux offers his own more modest republican sentiment: "How fine it would be to have no gates," he continues in his opposition not just to the Hunt gates but to kings and panjandrums everywhere, "to keep open House and trust all always."

∎∎∎

The history of the park is in many ways a tradition of creative compromise. Vaux defeats the grand entrance, but the fight isn't over. If not a grand entrance, the board proposes a high iron railing to encircle the grounds. Vaux exercising his skills at compromise persuades the board to accept the current low stone wall surrounding the park. In 1866 the board ratifies the

Currier & Ives. *Central Park, Winter—The Skating Pond* (1862). Metropolitan Museum of Art, bequest of Adele S. Colgate, 1962.

concept of four ungated portals along the southern boundary—meant, in language that Vaux might have proposed, to "extend to each citizen a rightful welcome." The rightful welcome proves a huge success when thousands of ice skaters arrive just as soon as the Pond opens in the winter of 1858. Ice skating in Central Park vaults to the top among New Yorkers' favorite outdoor activities, and soon it is even illuminated at night by calcium flares. Flares made of calcium oxide or quicklime, employed during the Civil War to illuminate military targets, were also employed in theaters during the 1860s and 1870s.[15] Nighttime skaters in Central Park are amateur actors, "in the limelight," contributing to a dramatic, but also implicitly political, scene of play. A Currier & Ives lithograph from 1862 shows men, women, and children on the frozen thirty-six-acre lake that soon becomes what Clarence Cook calls "the principal field for skaters in the Park."[16] There is even an area reserved for women skaters, if they prefer privacy. Newspapers praise skating as it expresses a model equality of conditions. "Masters Richard and William from Fifth Avenue, in their furs, and plain Dick and Bill from the avenues nearer the rivers, with bunting flying from joints and middle seams," as the *New York Herald* proclaims, "were all mingled in joyful unity."[17]

Unity, with Bow Bridge in the background like an emblem, is easier to proclaim than to achieve. The park as Walt Whitman describes it in 1879 is still a privileged ground for the upper classes. "Ten thousand vehicles careering through the Park this perfect afternoon," he writes. "Such a show! . . . Private barouches, cabs and coupés, some fine horseflesh—lapdogs, footmen, fashions, foreigners, cockades on hats, crests on panels—the full oceanic tide of New York's wealth and 'gentility.'"[18] The joyful unity in the Currier & Ives illustration does not include any skaters who are black. Master William and plain Bill are presumably both white. While a free state, New York is not entirely a safe haven for African Americans. The Fugitive Slave Law remains in force until 1864, and Frederick Douglass flees Manhattan at especially dangerous moments, which does not prevent him calling for court action to open New York schools to children of all races. Vaux in 1865 reminds Olmsted of their commitment to "the translation of the republican art idea in its highest form into the acres we want to control."[19]

Tocqueville has a surprising explanation, beyond ice skating or parks, for what accounts for the remarkable American equality of conditions: estate tax laws. "I am astonished," he marvels, "that ancient and modern political writers have not attributed to estate laws a greater influence on the course of human affairs."[20] American estate tax laws, he believes, break up the hereditary grip of landed aristocratic families in Europe. He might be equally astonished to learn that in the United States today the estate tax is all but revoked; in 2020 only 0.04 percent of all estates paid any estate tax. Central Park has nothing to do with inequities in the US tax code, but its attraction has much to do with its democratic values, reflected even in the low stone walls enclosing the park, which exist today only because Calvert Vaux defeated the panjandrum gates and negotiated a modest republican alternative. If some visitors can't afford $150 for a romantic sixty-minute carriage ride through the park, others are heartened that the carriage horses are now a concern of reformers who want humane treatment extended throughout the community of creatures in Central Park, nonhuman as well as human.

Central Park today, whatever its shortcomings, edges closer to fulfilling the purpose that Olmsted and Vaux envisioned in bridging economic and social differences. Dogs, off-leash at agreed-upon times, are as welcome as preschoolers. The Mall, no longer a grassy walkway for the fashionable elite, a showy promenade, is paved over to provide an all-weather, informal public emporium for street artists, musicians, and hucksters. Tourists still enjoy the shade of Olmsted's towering elms as they stroll along, stopping perhaps for a photo to prove they were there.

What does an equality of conditions look like today? June brides, perhaps foregoing pricey destination weddings, pose for photos beside the model boats sailing on Conservatory Water or host a reception under the trees. Ice cream, a low-cost populist favorite dating back to Olmsted's day, is available from handy vendor carts. Bridges and arches, thanks to Vaux, provide acoustic chambers for amateur musicians who busk for tips. A true equality of conditions remains a myth when income inequality in the United States is at an all-time high, but many aspects of the park aspire to equality just the same. In addition to a hint of Gilded Age opulence, the view from an 1893 illustration captures the remarkable sense of openness that Vaux fought for, as horse-drawn coaches and carriages leave or approach the southeast entrance to the park at Fifty-Ninth Street and Fifth Avenue. Central Park both in its ideals and in its shortcomings also offers much to consider when inequalities as well as political conflicts are directly and indirectly relevant to climate change.

ENTRANCE TO CENTRAL PARK, FIFTH AVENUE AND FIFTY-NINTH STREET.

Entrance to Central Park, Fifth Avenue and Fifty-Ninth Street (1893). New York Public Library Digital Collections.

The disasters spawned by rapidly changing weather patterns hit hardest among the poor, who usually live in areas where they are most exposed to the damage from degraded environments and from the fallout created by first-world carbon-based consumer economies. Whether you live in a trailer park or a mud hut, climate change is no fairytale and can, literally, blow your house down. The growing multitudes of homeless refugees and climate migrants have no shelter from the storms and shifts of a changing world. In a situation that looks hopeless at times, Central Park offers more than a metaphor to show that we can do better. It embodies principles of equality, the resolve, the hard work, and, strange as it may seem to say, the imagination we need to meet the unprecedented challenges of our time.

13

###

Imagination & Machinery

WHERE IS OLMSTED? What's he been doing? On January 22, 1861, while the nation is falling apart, he submits his letter of resignation to the Board of Commissioners in six crisp sentences.

It is a fateful year. On December 20, 1860, one month before Olmsted submits his letter to the board, South Carolina secedes from the Union. A handful of Southern states quickly follow. Dog-tired and now lame, walking with a cane after his near-death carriage accident, Olmsted has been working on the park almost four years straight, with only a brief leave of absence that was consumed in exhausting park-related travel. The trees he has planted in the lower park now need forty years to mature, while Andrew Green and the board continue to make his life miserable with their demand to cut costs. Lincoln in his first inaugural address on March 4, 1861, states the larger dilemma plainly. "I have no purpose, directly or indirectly," he says, "to interfere with the institution of slavery in the States where it exists. I believe I have no lawful right to do so, and I have no inclination to do so." Something has to give. The board president, adding additional uncertainty and stress, refuses to accept Frederick's letter of resignation.

Frederick, invited by the president to address the entire board, follows up his letter of resignation with a 13,000-word supplement: suspiciously more language than is required to resign. He pointedly declines to quarrel with Green, arguing instead that the "machinery" of the park is flawed:

"And the mending of the machinery, gentlemen," he concludes, "is your business, not mine."[1]

The board dithers for six months, deciding finally on a bizarre, untenable compromise: they accept his resignation as architect-in-chief but retain Olmsted as park superintendent, with a corresponding demotion in salary. Events, however, are beginning to spiral beyond the reach of compromise. On April 12, 1861, the South Carolina militia opens fire on the Union fort in Charleston Harbor. The nonstop artillery barrage creates a spectacular display of firepower that draws onlookers to rooftops and balconies. One day later the garrison at Fort Sumter surrenders, and the Civil War has begun. Frederick's life too is soon overturned.

Flawed machinery is a curious concept on which to rest his resignation from the post of architect-in-chief at Central Park. What does Olmsted mean? Machines are not new in Olmsted's day, but their social power is unprecedented. If the twentieth century runs on electricity, the nineteenth century is powered by steam. Steamboats in 1836 resemble almost mythic creatures for Emerson, as navigation is no longer, as in prior time immemorial, limited by winds or tides.[2] Thoreau is less sanguine as he hears the steam-driven train rattling past Walden Pond: "We do not ride on the railroad," he complains; "it rides upon us."[3] Olmsted employs the new steam-powered machines in Central Park wherever he can. He introduces the world's first mechanized stone crusher. Steam shovels dig out the New Reservoir, completing by 1862 a task that earlier would have taken years. Machinery, however, also holds a more abstract meaning for Olmsted, as reflected in his letter boasting that he has got the park working "like a machine." Johnson's famous *Dictionary* (1755) defines a machine as any complicated work in which one part contributes to the motion of another. Olmsted has organized and coordinated his multiple teams—gardeners, stonemasons, engineers, laborers, and the rest—like the wheels and pistons of a steam engine. The board, as he implies, fails to contribute its essential part to the coordinated motion of a perfect system.

Olmsted's extraordinary powers of organization, on public display at Central Park, are far more impressive in 1861 than his talents in landscape design.

Organizational powers are precisely what is needed when war breaks out. As his injured leg disqualifies him from military service, Olmsted looks for other ways to support the Union effort, even while continuing at Central Park in his lesser role as superintendent. *Supervision* is the term he comes to prefer when referring to the powers required to construct a smooth-running organization, and he even organizes and supervises a "home guard" that he recruits from the park police. They drill on Sundays. Much has changed in his personal life, however. He has an infant son at home—Mary gives birth to their first child in June 1860—and two books appear in quick succession: *A Journey in the Back Country* (1860) and his masterpiece, *The Cotton Kingdom* (1861). Circumstances have coalesced: exhaustion, conflict with the board, writing, and significant progress on the park. Most important, the nation is at war, North against South, and as he nears his fortieth birthday he cannot ignore the unprecedented danger to the republic.

It is two months after the assault on Fort Sumter. Events, age, emotions, family, and principles bring him, perhaps without his knowledge, to a turning point, when . . . opportunity knocks.

A prominent Unitarian minister who admires his writing on slavery comes to Olmsted with a proposal from the highest levels of government. A recently created wartime relief bureau—the United States Sanitary Commission (USSC)—needs a general secretary or, in modern terms, a chief executive officer. Would Olmsted be interested? The fledgling bureau is regarded as vital to the Union war effort, and Kairos doesn't offer second chances or time for reflection. On June 21, 1861, Olmsted accepts the new post as resident secretary, soon general secretary, of the new USSC. He is gone in a flash.

*　*　*

The name Sanitary Commission belies the bureau's crucial function. *Sanitas* in Latin means health, and the new USSC is modeled on the British Sanitary Commission, established during the Crimean War, which propelled Florence Nightingale to renown. Its mission is to provide civilian backup for the Medical Bureau of the War Department, and President Lincoln creates the USSC precisely because the Medical Bureau is clearly overtasked and underorganized, lacking the "machinery" needed to support the troops. The USSC raises money, sets up hospitals, oversees staffing, inspects hygiene at more than four hundred regimental camps, transports sick and wounded soldiers, and enlists thousands of volunteers, especially nurses. Mary in a letter tells Frederick that his appointment is a great honor. Always given to understatement, Frederick replies simply, "It is a good big work I have in hand."[4]

Big indeed. Olmsted has no credentials in medicine or military health. What he has in spades, however, is a proven ability to organize and to run successfully a large, complex organization. Clarence Cook in 1869—well before Central Park is complete—extends his praise of Olmsted's powers from the aesthetics of landscape to the mechanics of large and complex organizations. "Few Americans in our time," he writes, "have shown so great administrative abilities."[5]

Olmsted is no remote administrator. His title as general secretary belies his daily hands-on engagement. An army runs on its stomach, as the saying goes, but it goes nowhere with soldiers badly disabled by sickness and infection. More soldiers during the Civil War die from disease than from battlefield wounds. The USSC tends to sick and wounded soldiers both on the battlefield and in hospitals; it is responsible for inspecting military camp hygiene; and it runs some thirty rest homes or lodges for soldiers who are disabled. The Army of the Potomac looks badly overmatched during the chaotic six months after the attack on Fort Sumter, and the Union needs all the soldiers it can get and needs to keep them healthy. More than good hygiene is at issue. Exactly one month after Frederick assumes his new post at the USSC, Union soldiers are routed in Northern Virginia at the First Battle of Bull Run. They drop their rifles and flee toward Washington in panic, stoking widespread fears that the nation's capital is about to fall.

Olmsted in his new position receives personal visits from General George McClellan and from Edwin Stanton, the secretary of war. He also spends months on the road, an experienced traveler, helping to establish mobile forward aid stations, field hospitals, and general hospitals. The Sanitary Commission manages and coordinates an ever-shifting network of medical supplies, nurses, and doctors, but its most important life-saving responsibility is to transport wounded soldiers for care. Steamboats, locomotives, and horse-drawn ambulances, however, all face perpetual breakdowns, and failures in the machinery are not all organizational. Olmsted calls his exhausting daily work and travel with the USSC an "absorbing occupation" and a "connection with the work of the nation without which I should be very uncomfortable."[6] In October he meets with President Abraham Lincoln in Washington.

What about Central Park? Vaux remains in his position as assistant architect, overseeing construction. The division of responsibilities between Vaux and Olmsted has become over time a matter of mild contention or disagreement, which they rarely allow to escalate into outright conflict. One friendly division takes the form of a debate about whether Olmsted deserves the status of an artist. Vaux says that Olmstead is an artist, and Olmsted protests he isn't. The one occasion on which he claims an artist's role is when he supplements his initial letter of resignation, writing, somewhat tentatively, "I shall venture to assume to myself the title of artist."

Olmsted employs his claim largely as a bargaining chip in an implicit argument that he is indispensable. His artistic claims rest on the legitimate claim that he regularly exercises an artist's distinctive power of imagination. As he tells the board: "I mean that the best conceptions of scenery, the best plans, details of plans—intentions—the best, are not contrived by effort, but are spontaneous and instinctive." He instructs them, in a cut likely meant for Andrew Green, that in his role as the spontaneous park artist "there must be something which you can not buy in any market, of good quality, merely for money." He explains, as if addressing a conclave of iron-age philistines: "It is a natural, spontaneous, individual action of imagination—of creative fancy."[7]

Olmsted's feeling for nature and for the beauty of natural landscapes is not entirely a bargaining chip. It is evident as early as his experience at Birkenhead Park. "What artist, so noble, has often been my thought," he writes in *Walks and Talks*, "as he, who with far-reaching conception of beauty and designing power, sketches the outline, writes the colours, and directs the shadows of a picture so great that Nature shall be employed upon it for generations, before the work he has arranged for her shall realize his intentions."[8] This passage, however true to his feelings, also reads like a set piece of purple prose—and he likes it so well that he recycles the entire passage, verbatim, in his initial 1858 letter to the board accepting the position of architect-in-chief. Still, it reflects a consistent part of his psyche that he also consistently undervalues. Vaux, however, knows him better than he knows himself. "Mr. Vaux had a profound respect for Mr. Olmsted's constructive imagination and artistic power," writes Samuel Parsons, who knew Vaux well.[9] Olmsted at times can sound downright dismissive of artistic vision. "Landscape work," he once writes to Vaux, never seemed a way to make "a decent living."[10]

Imagination makes its strongest claim within Olmsted's at times divided self-understanding in his conviction that landscape design is *pictorial* in its methods and *emotional* in its purpose. It creates scenery and engages feelings. Landscapes in this sense belong to the province of art, but more often his thinking reflects a conflict in which imagination and organization tend to occupy opposing poles. In a retrospective letter about his childhood, he regrets the "strong natural propensity" that he indulged, as he puts it, "for roaming afield and day-dreaming under a tree." This tendency, he continues, left his mind "unfitted for close continuous, laborious application, as it remains today, so that at any moment . . . I am liable to lose the thread I wish to follow and go off wool-gathering."[11] *Wool-gathering* hardly expresses a visionary respect for the creative imagination. Perhaps, however, it is exactly a lofty esteem for art and artists that underlies his conflicting statements. "I don't feel myself an artist," he writes to Vaux: "I feel rather as if it was sacrilegious in me to post myself in the portals of Art." He describes himself as a practical man of action: "a hard worker and a doer."[12]

Vaux loses the struggle to adjust Olmsted's self-understanding, but in the process he offers an ingenious synthesis. Olmsted's distinctive powers, Vaux says, embrace both imagination *and* machinery, both artistic vision *and* a genius for organization. It is a rare combination. Vaux in fact sees in Olmsted an original and distinctively American version of the creative artist: a bold new figure who, in combining the contrary powers of practical organization and imaginative genius, represents a personification of the new republic.[13] Vaux may be right, but Olmsted is not convinced, or so he replies, and soon they tacitly agree to drop the subject.

███

"I was one of the few men in America," Olmsted writes in explaining how he came to install a small force of police-like "keepers" in Central Park, "who had made it a business to be well informed on the subject of police organization and management."[14]

A new era requires new artists—a thought worth considering in the era of climate change. Central Park surely requires an imaginative grasp of landscape design, but it also requires someone able to organize and to command a vast and diverse workforce. "Since the plan was adopted," Olmsted writes in 1860, "from two to four thousand men have been generally at work besides those employed by contractors." He adds: "there has been

Thomas Nast, *United States Sanitary Commission: Our Heroines. Harper's Weekly*, April 9, 1864.

the most perfect order, peace & good feeling preserved, notwithstanding the fact that the laborers are mainly from the poorest or what is generally considered the most dangerous class of the great city's population."[15] Tammany Hall, the organization that controlled Democratic politics in New York City during the construction of Central Park, was regularly described as a machine. Machinery as a metaphor can run counter to artistic ideas of free-flowing movement and improvisation. Worse, it can run counter to the personal, biological limits of human flesh and blood.

Katharine Prescott Wormeley as a young woman works closely with Olmsted at the USSC. English-born, living with her wealthy family in fashionable Newport, Rhode Island, she volunteers in the early days of the Civil War to serve as a nurse, afterward confirming both her remarkable talent and her tirelessness by translating the forty-volume complete works of Balzac. She and Olmsted are both novices in the new organization hastily stitched together in wartime, and her dedication helps instill in Olmsted a lasting respect for the contributions that women make to the lifesaving work of the USSC. Neither Wormeley nor Olmsted is trained for the work, however, and both work to the point of exhaustion. "I do not suffer under the sights," as she writes from the USSC steamship *Daniel Webster*; "but oh! the sounds, the screams of men."[16]

The screams are impossible to get used to, but Wormeley at least gets to observe Olmsted firsthand aboard the *Daniel Webster*. "The organizing genius of Mr. Frederick Law Olmsted," she writes, "made the Sanitary Commission what it practically became—a great machine running side by side with the Medical Bureau wherever the armies went." She adds: "He is a great organizer." On one unfortunately typical occasion she watches as 4,500 wounded men are simply dropped off at a USSC steamboat landing, with no surgeons and no one in charge. "You *can't conceive* what it is to stem the torrent of this disorder and utter want of organization," she writes: "Mr. Olmsted is everything—wise, authoritative, untiring; but he must break down."[17]

The breakdown took almost four years at Central Park, but in the Civil War it takes only twenty-seven months. Olmsted's talent for organization includes driving himself like a machine, until the machinery stops. He resigns as general secretary of the USSC on September 1, 1863, and—in a questionable therapy—immediately signs a five-year contract as manager with a California gold mining company. The position, hardly irrelevant for a man with a growing family and no job, pays five times his highest salary at Central Park.

Two weeks after resigning as head of the USSC and bound for San Francisco, he boards a ship and is gone again.

14

███

Big Artwork of the Republic

"I AM FOR THE PRESENT making money pretty fast for such a vagabond as I am," Frederick writes to his father from California, somewhat proudly, in 1864.[1] The Mariposa Company hires him as the manager of a gold mining operation. He is not entirely pleased, despite his new funds, with the landscape or the people. "I hate the wilderness & wild, tempestuous, gambling men, such as I shall have to master," as he tells Mary.[2] He reports that within days of his arrival two men are killed with knives. The workers soon go on strike when he cuts wages at the mines, and violence follows when he breaks the strike with replacements. It is easy to believe that he thinks back fondly at times to Central Park and to the civilized questions it raises concerning openness, escape, machinery, and art.

It is Calvert Vaux in a letter to Olmsted who describes Central Park in 1864 as "the big artwork of the Republic."[3] The claim, while doubtless sincere, raises immediate questions. First, can a park *be* an artwork? Second, what do we mean by *art*? Third, can any artwork in any medium—from *Moby-Dick* to *American Gothic*—stand as *the* supreme representative of the nation's cultural and political values? Central Park at least embodies values, however hard to articulate, that set it far apart from, say, a random patch of urban greenspace. The affection that visitors feel for Central Park can't simply express a value-free, meaningless spasm in the limbic system. Art has a traditional role in moving emotion and embodying values, even contradictory values or values that we cannot raise to consciousness.

"What thou lovest well remains," writes poet Ezra Pound during another war, "the rest is dross." A "national treasure" is what Eugene Kinkead, longtime staff writer and editor at *The New Yorker*, calls Central Park.[4] "Central Park as a Work of Art" is the subtitle of a collection of Olmsted's papers coedited by his son, Frederick Law Olmsted Jr.[5] Suppose, despite all the unanswered questions and all the reasonable objections, is it possible, just possible, that Vaux could be right.

⚏

Olmsted at least once entertains the idea that Central Park is a work of art. "For the next century it must be held a work of Art, or a failure," he writes about Central Park.[6] His meaning is not self-evident, but it likely acknowledges that no one knows what the next century will bring. Trees will die, tastes will change, his living picture may fade. Who knows? At least for the immediate future, however, Olmsted implies that Central Park is indeed a work of art. The open question is only whether it is judged a successful or unsuccessful artwork. If he and Vaux are right, two features make the park distinctive as even a presumptive artwork. First, people are essential to the work as participants, actors rather than audience. Second, it is an artwork that contains other artworks. Nature provides the raw organic materials as the soil warms and photosynthetic processes turn the leaves green. The artful arrangement of trees, shrubs, ponds, and terrain, however, also and simultaneously creates an artistic container—like an 843-acre museum—for the display and performance of other works of art.

Vaux pointedly reminds Olmsted of their joint decision in devising the Greensward plan to view the park "as a vital organism to be artistically treated."[7] Central Park as a living artwork is distinctive in the sense that people are intrinsic components—not *objects* of representation, as in a painting or on the stage, but rather active *participants*. The parkgoers are part of the dramatic action. Their coming and going is the human systole and diastole of the living artwork. They move about in a continuous flow during daylight hours, and on summer evenings they often return after dark for public concerts. The few midnight hours when everyone is gone simply provide an intermission before the birds awaken, sounds commence, and the first runners arrive. The people and land together define a living organic ensemble that has no single creator but constitutes a collaborative, changing, cross-generational artwork.

People, at least in America, also constitute a political force that Central Park interweaves into the artwork as a locus of value. It is Vaux, sometimes a bit impatient with Olmsted's focus on machine-like organization, who sees Central Park as a material opportunity to "translate Democratic ideas into Trees & Dirt."[8]

Central Park as a container for other works of art poses serious questions for the new age of climate change as it challenges, if indirectly, the traditional binary split between nature and art. It also challenges the equally troubling binary split between people and nature. Central Park moreover not only *contains* numberless organic life forms—vegetation, visitors, scarlet tanagers, and red-tailed hawks—but also seethes with life even when it might appear immobile, as on a subzero winter morning when the grass covering the Great Lawn turns white with frost. The stillness is illusory. Suddenly a sparrow darts out in search of berries or a crow knocks a puff of snow from the life-size statue of Shakespeare on the Mall.

"It has been said many times," writes Samuel Parsons in 1919, "that Central Park is the greatest artistic treasure owned by the citizens of New York."[9] New Yorkers do not truly *own* Central Park, of course, except in the same technical or legal sense that they own the Verrazzano-Narrows Bridge. Parsons, however, is not a lone rogue voice. "Central Park is not only a shining example of outdoor design," claims a 2022 article in the *Wall Street Journal*, "but also one of the greatest works of American art."[10] Central Park doubtless could be described today as a work of environmental art or earth art, but it is an unusual variation: not an object, however material, but a living organism in which trees and boulders share space with an open-ended chain of city dogs taking their humans for a walk.

Central Park gets away with stretching—even vaporizing—the traditional claim that great works of art are, by definition, timeless. Time, however, is built into the structure and fabric of Central Park. Countless insects, fish, and migrating birds pass by, mostly unseen, although I once watched a water turtle dig a nest for her eggs. Three thousand cubic yards of leaves fall each year, all returned to the park now in a continuous compost operation along with another five thousand cubic yards of waste: an unseen cycle of life.[11] The park is timeless only in the sense that a waterfall can appear frozen in perpetual motion. Even the solid statues and sculptures, rooted in concrete, slowly come and go from their pedestals as tastes change or as the times demand, like the pollution-based threats to remove Cleopatra's Needle. Amateur musicians performing under a wide arch for maximum vibrato rarely stay for long, although some seem to play regular gigs. Central Park also contains a professional open-air theater, added in 1962 and now under renovation. Everything seems to change, and it's anyone's guess what unimagined new media will find a temporary home in the future park.

▮▮▮

Scenery is the term that Olmsted consistently uses in ways that associate park-making with art. Painting, especially picturesque art, is of course basic to his work in Central Park, but it is scenery—not a particular style—that for Olmsted defines a park. "I reserve the word *park*," he writes, "for places with breadth and space enough, and with all other needed qualities to justify the application to what you find in them of the word *scenery*." Parks, he adds, belong to "the art of landscape or scenery-making."[12]

Scenery in parks also serves a purpose for Olmsted independent from its uses in painting and theater. It is not a setting or backdrop but the main action. It is an action that not only transforms visitors into participants but also changes the participants through their engagement in the action. Thus he emphasizes how Central Park achieves its effects "by means of scenes through observation of which the mind may be more or less lifted out of moods and habits into which it is, under the ordinary conditions of life in the city, likely to fall."[13] He quotes Emerson's view that nature "soothes and sympathizes."[14] Natural scenery, unlike theater props that represent locations, entails an implicit biopoetics of solace and consolation, elevating the mood if we are feeling low, or adding to our sadness on a dark and rainy day. The positive role of scenery in orchestrating our moods—making life in the city, as Olmsted puts it, happier and healthier—is what he calls the "main object and justification" of an urban park.

The differences between Olmsted and Vaux begin to widen over the idea of scenery. Scenery for Vaux *includes* buildings. Thus, while he shares Olmsted's passion for landscape scenes, he does not share Olmsted's view that buildings detract from the park, and the new permanent home for the Metropolitan Museum of Art, for which he designs the original building, bites off ten acres of prime parkland. Belvedere Castle too is a decorative folly, which he designs together with Jacob Wrey Mould. It deducts a smaller but more prominent chunk of land—the second highest elevation in the park—and offers little beyond a bogus, if charming, contribution to the scenery. Don't try to book a room. It's all a solid fake. The doors and windows are always open to the weather.

Detail, Delacorte Theater, Central Park (July 2021). Rhododendrites, Creative Commons License.

Belvedere Castle is just barely visible peeking behind the Delacorte Theater, where the stage set depicts a New York City neighborhood created for a 2021 production of *The Merry Wives of Windsor*. The play was first performed for Queen Elizabeth about 1597, as rumor has it, but the scenery or stage set in this performance situates Shakespeare's play in a South Harlem neighborhood mostly populated by African immigrants.[15] The photograph captures the traditional third-wall separation between actors and audience, but the split is in one sense as illusory as Belvedere Castle. The audience is indeed separate from the play, but the audience is also absorbed, like the play, *within* the park. The park as artwork not only contains the play but contains the people, not only as audience but as participants in the life of the park, whose feelings for the play and the park belong as securely to the artwork as rock-solid Belvedere Castle.

Central Park is spacious enough to enfold almost whatever definition of art you prefer. For Olmsted, the art of the park performs its function best when it quiets the mind and induces a meditative, poetic state. The art of the park for me, on the other hand, offers entry into a sort of urban sanctuary or asylum. *Asylum* in its Greek root refers to the legal right of immunity from seizure, often in a temple or sacred grove, and a *sanctuary* too emphasizes the act of entry into a protected zone. Entering into a sanctuary is thus not quite the same action as opening a door to enter a room. The entry into a sanctuary initiates a change of condition, legal for the ancient world and psychological for me. Entering into Central

Park feels less like a freedom from seizure than like a homecoming. The terrain seems strangely familiar, even when I stumble into unfamiliar areas of the Ramble that I've never seen before. I'm not alone in feeling oddly reconnected. Barack Obama in 2012, during his second presidential campaign, goes so far as to propose wearing a fake moustache so he can stroll through the park, undisturbed. "You know, I just desperately want to take a walk through Central Park again," he recalls pleading with his Secret Service cohort, "and just remember what it feels like."[16] What he wants to remember, which surprises me but reflects his finest qualities, is not a place but a *feeling*. The agents of course turn him down.

■■■

Central Park as an artwork containing other artworks opens up an inquiry that ranges from the obvious presence of statues and sculptures—which Olmsted and Vaux discourage—to installations that subtly reflect back upon the artwork that contains them. In February 2005, suddenly, 7,503 large saffron-orange nylon curtains appear to march across twenty miles of snow-dusted paths. Bulgarian-born artist Christo and his French-born wife Jeanne-Claude title their enigmatic work *The Gates*. Christo and Jeanne-Claude, who both use single names in their work, say that *The Gates* draws inspiration from the *torii* gates associated with traditional Shinto shrines in Japan. *Torii* gates evoke a sacred bond between the land and its inhabitants, although Christo and Jeanne-Claude imagine resonances from heaven's gates to the gates of paradise. Christo also mentions the gates or gaps in the low wall that surrounds Central Park. *The Gates* as a visual artwork, beyond its resonances, invites New Yorkers to reencounter the familiar park as strangely defamiliarized. Pleased or simply puzzled, multitudes walk beneath bright orange curtains in an experience that cannot resemble the detachment of spectators watching a parade, fenced off on the sidewalk. The walkers are not merely "in" the park, in a geographical sense, but many say they enter into an altered state of awareness. They are *part* of the park, active participants too walking within a bizarre orange artwork that somehow reconnects them with the park and with its magic. Some people say in interviews that they feel as if they have entered into a mystery: an enigmatic realm they don't understand. Christo insists on the essential purposelessness of *The Gates*. Like a parable, its meaning—uncontrolled by artists or critics—is ultimately ungraspable.

The Gates as an artwork shares with the park that contains it several key features: it is exceptionally large, fundamentally gratuitous, and intellectually uncontainable. It overflows whatever meaning or purpose might be imposed to explain or contain it, and it simply opens up or unfolds like an excessive and unreasonable gift that you can't really understand and can't return. It simply *is*.

Christo and Jeanne-Claude enjoy injecting a transient jolt of play and surprise into our everyday lives. The orange curtains billowing in the breeze and secured by heavy steel frames vanish almost as suddenly as they arrived. The work, by design, is ephemeral: it includes its own disappearance. *The Gates* in what Christo calls its "hardware phase" remains in place for only two weeks before the colorful fabric comes down—metal frames disassembled, screws and bolts recycled, fabric repurposed—in a planned disappearance that is utterly unlike the cerebral disembodiment of conceptual art. There is, apparently, *no* concept. *The Gates* simply comes into being after more than twenty-six years of planning, the "software" phase, and then one day it no longer exists. It is not clear how to understand what has just happened. "I don't know if I'm successful," Christo says, playing with ideas of success, "but all my works, they are suicidal in some way."[17]

"If the stars should appear one night in a thousand years," Emerson writes, "how would men believe and adore; and preserve for many generations the remembrance of the city of God which had been shown!"[18] Emerson's image seeks to remind readers of the sacred or spiritual mysteries of nature that they ignore in going about their daily tasks. Christo imagines a similar, if more secular, impact for *The Gates*: "You can say to

Carol M. Highsmith, The Gates, a Site-Specific Work of Art by Christo and Jeanne-Claude in Central Park, New York City (2005). Library of Congress.

your grandson, I saw that, that was once there, but never again." *The Gates* reenchants a familiar landmark much as a one-time reappearance of the stars might reenchant the night sky. "All our projects have this type of quality," Christo says, "that if you missed it, you will never see them." As he says about *The Gates* in its evanescence: "Once in a lifetime, if never again."[19]

▟▟▟

Central Park, while it absorbs artworks and artistic performances, includes one genre that Olmsted and Vaux generally disapprove of. Clarence Cook, whom they both know well, likely reflects their view in cautioning against interrupting the pastoral scenery of the park with miscellaneous distractions. "The great danger," he warns, "is, lest the Park should come to be looked upon merely as a place wherein are collected a large number of curious and rare, or pretty things, which would, it is true, be a recommendation to a museum, or to a garden of plants or animals, but is not proper to a park."[20] No matter. Friedrich Schiller thus as early as 1859 receives the first statue, thanks to a gift from German-speaking New Yorkers, while Poland in 1945 adds a giant equestrian statue of its fifteenth-century hero King Jagiełło, I'm not sure why. Shakespeare and Robert Burns may deserve statues on the Mall as national bards revered by groups of Anglo-Americans, but what about Fitz-Greene Halleck? Halleck, born in 1790, has been called "the most famous gay poet you've never heard of." President Rutherford B. Hayes unveils Halleck's statue in 1877 before a cheering crowd of ten thousand spectators so unruly that New York passes an ordinance to limit the size of future events.[21] Even runners erect a statue to their patron saint, Fred Lebow, cofounder of the New York City Marathon. The finish line, a ceremonial scene of achievement as much as a mile marker, is always placed in Central Park.

Central Park today contains twenty-nine statues, including figures as diverse as Beethoven, Simón Bolívar, and Mother Goose.[22] No statue is more famous, however, than Emma Stebbins's *Angel of the Waters*, unveiled in 1873. The giant angel constitutes a showpiece atop the central fountain that anchors Bethesda Terrace. The first public artwork in New York City commissioned from a woman, the *Angel of the Waters* now finds a worthy companion in the Women's Rights Pioneers Monument, erected in 2020, commemorating ratification of the Nineteenth Amendment, which gives women the right to vote, depicting Sojourner Truth, Susan B. Anthony, and Elizabeth Cady Stanton. New statues stand as a reminder that Central Park remains in active dialogue with the changing times. The story of Cleopatra's Needle in fact does not conclude with the nineteenth-century colonial politics that brings it to the park. Egypt now threatens to take the obelisk back unless New York City quickly protects it from decades of acid rain and urban pollutants.

The parade of statues is potentially endless, which helps explain why Olmsted and Vaux mostly resist them. Mostly. They make one significant exception, soliciting donations to fund a bust of Andrew Jackson Downing. When only seven donors respond, Vaux does perhaps the next best thing to honor his benefactor, partner, friend, and kindred spirit. He names his second son Downing.

Time is a cradle of ironies from which Central Park, as a living artwork, cannot claim exemption. The Metropolitan Museum of Art today contains only a small fragment of the building that Vaux originally designed, now swallowed up under acres of indifferent roof. Andrew Green never receives an honorary statue, which Olmsted fans might call poetic justice. In 1929 he does receive a granite bench, later relocated across from the composting area. Balto the sled dog does far better, receiving a much-loved and child-climbed statue for his role in 1925—likely unknown to most climbers—bringing vital diphtheria antitoxin to Nome, Alaska. Clearly, Olmsted's contemporaries and subsequent generations do not share his preference for undisturbed park scenery. Central Park includes life-size statues of miscellaneous historical celebrities from Alexander Hamilton to Hans Christian Andersen. Unaccountably, there is no statue of Calvert Vaux and—even worse—no statue of Frederick Law Olmsted.

⦙⦙⦙

Olmsted late in life allows himself to take credit for raising landscape architecture from a trade to a "liberal profession" and an "Art."[23] He lives long enough to correspond with Mariana Griswold Van Rensselaer (1851–1934), the first American woman who publishes as an architectural critic. She describes him in *Art Out-Of-Doors* (1893) as the most remarkable artist yet born in America.[24] Olmsted's status as artist and the status of Central Park as an artwork are always open to argument, of course, but the discussion takes on new focus and new meaning as we rethink our relations with the earth in the age of global climate change. Parks, especially urban parks, have a changed role to play when melting ice caps inexorably raise sea levels and when atmospheric rivers flood the land. Can we continue to take the position of *outsiders*, of mere stewards or managers of nature? Or could parks help us reimagine our role as *participants* inseparable from the natural world? "This is a delicious evening," Thoreau writes in a chapter of *Walden* entitled (perhaps with his usual sense of irony) "Solitude." He is anything but alone. This particular evening, he continues, is a time "when the whole body is one sense, and imbibes delight through every pore. I go and come with a strange liberty in Nature, a part of herself. As I walk along the stony shore of the pond in my shirt sleeves . . . all the elements are unusually congenial to me. The bullfrogs trump to usher in the night, and the note of the whippoorwill is borne on the rippling wind from over the water. Sympathy with the fluttering alder and poplar leaves almost takes away my breath."[25]

I just don't find Andy Warhol's soup cans or Jeff Koons's balloon dogs breathtaking. Interesting, yes, but not *breathtaking*. As I enter Central Park, exiting the steady rumble of traffic on Fifth Avenue all the way north to the Guggenheim Museum, I experience a calm sense of belonging that almost takes my breath away.

15

Decline & Renewal

"I DON'T KNOW what's the matter. I no sooner get pen to paper than a horrid sort of nightmare begins to grow upon me, and the longer I write the worse it gets, till finally my eyes twitch and I have to quit to avoid suffocation."[1] Frederick's state of body and mind, as reflected in this letter from California on Christmas Day 1863, does not appear promising. The California gold-rush of the early 1850s is over. Gunshots are endemic. "The natural death of the country is cold lead in the brain," he writes dryly a few months earlier.[2] The jaunty boast to his father—that he is making money "pretty fast"—may well feel empty.[3] Homesickness, nightmares, failing eyesight, temporary writer's block, and feelings of suffocation hardly suggest a happy arrival in the West. Soon, however, it gets even worse.

Nine months later, in January 1865, the entire Mariposa Company goes bankrupt.[4]

The collapse of the Mariposa Company costs Frederick his job and also entangles him in claims of financial mismanagement. A federal commissioner absolves him of crime, describing him in an official document as honest but inept. *Inept?* Olmsted is a man with an overwork ethic who is accustomed to think well of himself. "I *know* that I have unusual abilities," he writes while contemplating the move to California, "unusual, far reaching sagacity."[5] "I believe he sees out of the back of his head occasionally," writes Katharine Wormeley recalling the early days of the USSC.[6] He feels temporarily buoyed in April 1865 by news that General Lee has surrendered, but five days later the assassination of Lincoln leaves him sapped of emotion. "At any rate the nation lives and is immortal and Slavery is dead," he writes: "Enough for us."[7] The stress takes a toll in illness and depression.

▮▮▮

Vaux comes to the rescue once again. Out of the blue, Olmsted receives a letter from the Broadway firm of Vaux & Withers, Architects. It is from Calvert Vaux and begins "Dear Olmsted." Although brief, the letter is a cautious opening in a campaign to lure Olmsted east to work with Vaux on a commission to design Brooklyn's new Prospect Park. Vaux needs to avoid a direct invitation, which runs the risk that Olmsted will immediately turn him down. "I wish you could have seen your destiny in our art," the letter continues with just a modest risk. A slow-motion dance has nonetheless begun as their exchange of letters takes its slow journey across the country by coach and rail. Each man has grievances to air, however delicately, and explanations to supply at great length. Not yet biting on the idea of a return, Olmsted mentions unspecified business that keeps him in San Francisco, where he is nonetheless friendless, depressed, and alone. "Never say die," Vaux urges cheerfully, "we may have some fun together yet."[8]

Olmsted, now directionless, dispirited, desperately in search of funds, has spent two years in California, two years at the USSC, and four exhausting years at Central Park. After nearly a decade, in his early forties, married with four children, and stranded on the West Coast, he seems to have run out of options. The sublime scenery of Yosemite offers some solace, and he pours his energy into a report to Congress supporting a decision to make Yosemite a national reserve—support that will later help underwrite the new system of national parks. But he is, for all his unusual abilities, a man who for the first time in his vagabond life seems genuinely lost.

Vaux is relentless. Without Vaux in 1858, there is no Greensward plan and no appointment for Olmsted as architect-in-chief at Central Park. Without Vaux in 1865, Olmsted's vagabond career might have reached the end of the road in Bear Valley, California. Olmsted after a few face-saving months of deliberation agrees to return to New York. "My heart really bounds (if you don't mind poetry) to your suggestion that we might work together," he writes to Vaux with his decision.[9] Is he recalling Wordsworth? Olmsted elsewhere quotes a passage from "Tintern Abbey" in which Wordsworth describes his wandering childhood education in nature. The quotation might also describe what Olmsted calls his own "vagabond life."[10]

Olmsted and Vaux at Prospect Park create what some authorities consider an even more impressive feat of landscape art than Central Park. They also formalize a truly equal partnership by creating the new landscape firm of Olmsted, Vaux & Company. Their partnership lasts seven years, longer than some rock groups and marriages. It is an amicable parting when they dissolve the firm to pursue independent ventures, Olmsted relocating to Boston and Vaux remaining in New York City. They occasionally reunite in an intermittent advisory role at Central Park, and in 1871 they actively promote the appointment of Frederic Church to the Central Park Board of Commissioners. They believe that Church as patriarch of the Hudson River School of painting will maintain the board's commitment to what Olmsted calls the "art element."[11] The recruitment of Church is not a random stroke of luck. Vaux is working directly with him in designing the Church family mansion, Olana.

"The park is alive," writes Samuel Parsons in 1919, "an organism of vegetation constructed on a definite artistic plan which naturally is continually decaying and then continually, by one means or another, recreating itself."[12] Parsons succeeds Vaux as the new head landscape architect of New York City, and his opinion carries weight. He is of course expanding on the view shared by Olmsted and Vaux that Central Park is a living organism, but his emphasis on decay and renewal adds a significant twist. Central Park as a living organism is necessarily engaged in cycles of growth and decline. Decline, while inevitable in an open system of living organisms, does not automatically assure renewal.

"The Park has suffered great injury," Olmsted writes in 1872.[13] He is back in New York City, visiting from Boston. He sees his evergreens, so carefully planted, now clumped tightly together as evidence that the board has forgotten or overlooked a long-term regimen of thinning and replanting. Olmsted chooses his words carefully. *Injury* as a legal term implies culpable neglect. Even now, he continues, the park cannot wholly recover from "the neglect of the plantations and the maltreatment of the last year and a half." The park, he writes, looks "slovenly and neglected." The Department of Public Parks in its annual report for 1871–1872 bears out his complaint. Park "keepers"—the policing force that Olmsted proudly instituted—have disappeared. Prostitutes and tramps have taken up residence in the park, according to local newspapers. Olmsted seems most disturbed that the park's landscape office has adopted the European fad for a sculpted appearance. As he writes with sarcastic scorn, it makes the park look as "natty as a new silk hat."[14] The rage for order can produce forms of disorder and decline whose machine-tooled power to destroy we are just starting to recognize.

"Nature is thoroughly mediate," Emerson writes in *Nature* (1836). "It is made to serve." He continues: "It receives the dominion of man as meekly as the ass on which the Saviour rode."[15] His language alludes to the biblical passage in which God gives Adam "dominion" over all living creatures (Genesis 1:26). Nature, Emerson claims, "offers all its kingdoms to man as the raw material which he may mould into what is useful. Man is never weary of working it up." His future-oriented confidence in the dominion of mankind over nature extends to his enthusiasm for steamships and railroads. Satellite images today show the United States lit up at night like an advertisement for fossil fuels. Central Park, by contrast, appears in a NASA photo of Manhattan from 2013 as a long, slim, dark rectangle. It suggests that a massive park, even if worked up by human art, can embody a wisdom that relinquishes, while it critiques, a dominion over the natural world.

Descartes, writing at the seventeenth-century origin of the scientific and industrial revolutions, famously asserts that science has transformed

Detail, Earth observations taken by the Expedition 35 Crew (2013). Courtesy of NASA, iss035e008051.

humankind into the "masters" and "possessors" of nature.[16] Recent environmental disasters suggest that nature still has the upper hand, despite our skill at producing new CO_2-generating explosives.[17] Would it be wiser to see ourselves not as masters, managers, and stewards but as *participants* and *protectors*? As protectors, we might openly acknowledge our position *within* nature—acting as families do to protect family members—not outsiders allotting resources and plotting to colonize even outer space. Despite star wars, drones, and moonshots, we belong to the kinship of earthbound creatures—two-legged, four-legged, winged, or finned—and it would seem wise to protect our family on home ground before decline becomes extinction.

Central Park offers a miniature laboratory for understanding decline and possible renewal. The decline of the park that Olmsted laments in 1872 follows failures in the body politic. In May 1870 the state legislature returns control of Central Park to the mayor of New York City, and it becomes in effect a patronage machine under the corrupt Democratic Party capo William M. Tweed. "Boss" Tweed in 1870 replaces the original eleven-member Board of Commissioners with a five-member substitute headed by, yes, Andrew Green. Olmsted and Vaux, in unison, immediately resign from their advisory roles, returning only after the fall of the Tweed Ring in 1877. The lasting damage, however, is already done and a steady decline ensues. Central Park for almost the next hundred years remains, as historian Walter Karp puts it, "in the hands of men more or less hostile to the spirit that created it."[18]

Central Park, absent the protection of Vaux and Olmsted, no longer resembles even a natty silk hat, and any resemblance to a picturesque landscape is long gone. When another financial crisis in the 1970s slashes half its budget, Central Park loses half its staff. Rains turn the Great Lawn into mud, beer cans litter the Pond, Bethesda Terrace plays host to drug deals, and visitors who linger after dusk almost beg to be mugged. The *New York Times* in 1977 notes the absence of any organized police response to assaults, peddling, narcotics, and even "dogs running wild."[19] Vandalism forces Belvedere Castle to shut down. Entropy alone is not at work. The human-created and politically motivated declines entail the power of their own reversal, which offers a hopeful sign for the era of climate change. Collective human action has also led since 1980 to an inspiring renewal of Central Park.

Central Park is "on the brink of collapse," recalls Elizabeth Barlow Rogers, when she takes on a position as "leader of the cause to save it from destruction."[20] Rogers's campaign, which many at first regard as "quixotic," succeeds not only in reviving Central Park but also, equally important, in creating an innovative, exportable model of public-private partnerships.[21] The Central Park Conservancy (CPC) which, Olmsted-like, she brings into being, is a well-funded private nonprofit organization that now shares joint responsibility for Central Park. New York City pays a portion of the annual budget, and the CPC supplies the rest. The partnership, founded in 1980, creates new private sources of funding that allow the Conservancy to employ specialists in soils, hydrology, geology, vegetation, and ecology. Together they begin to rethink how different groups use the park, including walkers, drivers, and even horseback riders. Most important, Rogers and her CPC teams understand the park as an organic creation in which nature and culture intermingle in changing patterns, not a static artifact or a picture that might be restored to some distant original state.[22] There is no original state of Central Park. No return to the Greensward vision. No picturesque landscape. No return to piggeries and bone-boiling stench. Only change.

The Central Park Conservancy now has around a $200 million endowment, which it supplements with regular fund drives and other money-raising projects, and it also assumes all day-to-day operations and staffing required to maintain the park. The city in turn retains authority over permits and events. The Great Lawn, no longer an oval dirtscape one rain away from turning into a giant pool of mud, is now a lush green field, protected with temporary flooring for outdoor concerts. The metal plaques backing the handy park benches provide another source of revenue to assure a continuing renewal. Emma Stebbins's *Angel of the Waters*, as overflow from the fountain cascades into the basin below, provides an appropriate setting and a fitting symbol of renewal when John A. Paulson announces a whopping $100 million gift to the CPC. The gift has its origin in the sketchy 1970s, when Paulson used to hang out with his teenage pals beside the fountain, which, as the *New York Times* reports, "was then scrawled with graffiti and bone dry."[23]

Time is running out for renewal as the global decline advances. The Thwaites ("Doomsday") Glacier in West Antarctica is the size of Florida, and its disappearance means that sea levels will rise perilously as warm ocean currents rush miles beneath its surface.[24] Some 40 percent of the world's population must somehow move fast to higher ground—or die. Many climate refugees are already dying in parched deserts and on choppy seas. The World Bank in 2018 says that by 2050 Latin America, sub-Saharan Africa, and Southeast Asia will generate 143 million more climate migrants. A world of desperate climate migrants, with more than three million in the United States alone as of 2023, is not a world we want to bequeath to our children.[25]

"In short," summarizes UN Secretary-General António Guterres, "our world needs climate action on all fronts—everything, everywhere, all at once."[26] Ten thousand new "people's parks" won't solve the climate crisis. The climate crisis, however, is less a puzzle to solve, as if there were a missing piece to discover, than a worldwide dilemma that we must enter into and address. The United Nations Environment Program has assisted in more than seventy-five projects in more than fifty countries on adaptation to climate change: projects aimed to benefit some 2.7 million people, to restore over 300,000 acres of land, to improve knowledge of how to adapt, and to construct more than 1,100 water harvesting structures.[27] Significant work goes on without media fanfare. Ten thousand Central Parks, as a fantasy project, might well provide a hopeful symbol if it succeeds in focusing attention, raising awareness, and inspiring effective action.

This may be exactly the right moment for a high-profile, unifying project similar to President John F. Kennedy's 1961 challenge to put an American on the moon. Fans of Central Park need not imagine replicating 843-acre monoliths. So-called pocket parks offer a promising alternative in replanting urban plots with native trees and shrubs, as is already under way in cities from Kraków to Kuala Lumpur. The impact, beyond cosmetic change, can be measured in reduced crime, disrupted heat islands, and increased neighborhood cohesion. New city parks in the thousands constitute a climate-changing project that aims to engage local populations in turning areas of urban decline into health-affirming greenspace. Serving life, whatever it meant to Nietzsche, must now mean serving not only human lives, including the lives of future generations, but also—crucially—*all* life: flora, fauna, rivers, mountains, and the damaged seas that cover 70 percent of the surface of the earth. Parks, while a small fraction of the land, can have a big impact on cities, and they can serve as a powerful metaphor for the reciprocity between humans and the life of the planet that we must, in our self-interest, learn how to protect.

Renewal also suggests that in addressing decline and in serving life we can also make amends. "Give me your hands / If we be friends," says the mischief-maker Puck at the conclusion of *A Midsummer Night's Dream*, "and Robin shall restore amends." Making amends is a crucial step for recovering alcoholics, and parks too offer an opportunity to make amends.

"This is righting a wrong," says Elizabeth Smith, who since 2018 has served as president of the CPC. She is referring to a $160 million project for renewal on the northern boundary of Central Park.[28] This boundary abuts East Harlem, and the new project will create a landscape designed as especially open and welcoming to neighboring minorities. "What was here," Smith says, "divided the park and kept East Harlem residents from enjoying the rest of the park." Known as the Harlem Meer Center, the project will create a new swimming pool that doubles in winter as a skating rink. An underground stream, excavated and rerouted, will meander amid meadows and sloping hillsides. A local landscape architect rightly describes its spirit as "Olmstedian."

"Vauxian" too, of course, and not only in its architectural features. In making amends, the Harlem Meer Center honors the democratic spirit of inclusiveness that underlies what Olmsted and Vaux regarded as a people's park. It gives something back of what was lost in Seneca Village. We may not always be able to prevent loss, as new public parks displace homes built in flood plains, but we can remember and honor those who sacrifice for the greater public good.

▪▪▪

"There is no other place in the world that is as much home to me," Olmsted writes about Central Park. He is writing to Vaux from California in 1865, after an absence of three years, and his affection for Central Park is more than casual or unthinking. "I love it all through & all the more for the trials it has cost me."[29] It seems fitting, in what becomes a lifetime of travels, that he singles out Central Park as his spiritual home. He is hardly alone. Central Park seems endowed with a power to draw visitors as if it constituted an archetypal green world safe and ideal for daydreaming or wandering or just sitting on a bench. It is not just a place but a psychic space we carry within that holds memories perhaps of childhood or home.

Wayfarer, Olmsted's earliest pen name, remains a good one-word description of the man who spends a lifetime in travels but finds no place as homelike as Central Park. Decline, however, is not aways open to renewal and amends. I sense a hint of elegiac sadness in the portrait by his celebrated fellow Bostonian John Singer Sargent, who depicts Frederick in his seventies, looking old and worn-out, as he appears to emerge from the landscape he designed for the North Carolina estate of a rich Vanderbilt

John Singer Sargent, *Frederick Law Olmsted* (1895). Used with permission from The Biltmore Company, Asheville, North Carolina.

grandson, his last commission. The foliage is invented. Sargent, best known for his portraits of "society" figures, adds the generic laurel-dogwood-rhododendron background only after he returns to his studio, in a break from his usual practice. Olmsted, now unwell, leaves before the Sargent has finished the painting, perhaps showing signs of the dementia that family members prefer to ignore, concerned for his reputation, his legacy, and the family business. Anecdotes suggest that Sargent is not pleased when Olmsted exits early. The portrait creates an image in which Olmsted appears almost in need of an escape from nature. His back is turned to the single small patch of open sky.

Ecosystems and species are more resilient than individuals, who decline and die a natural death if not struck down prematurely. Earth has absorbed mass extinctions that took millions of years to repair, but individuals get only a limited lifespan in which to make their mark. In 1898, when Mary can no longer care for him, Olmsted is admitted as a patient to the McLean Asylum in Belmont, Massachusetts, where he had once submitted a design for the grounds and where he dies in 1903. He leaves his mark, however, in a legacy that stretches from 843 acres of urban greenspace to models of collaboration, risk-taking, thinking big, and seizing opportunities. The question, hardly rhetorical, is what mark will *we* leave?

CONCLUSION

The Fullness of Life

Analogy, comparison, indirection, suggestions are perhaps all that is possible.
—Walt Whitman, "Sunday Evening Lectures" (1899)

"I had no more idea of ever being a park-maker," Olmsted once writes re-flecting on his visit to London in 1856 as editor for Dix, Edwards & Company, "than of taking command of the Channel fleet."[1] He did not count on Calvert Vaux. The hidden power of collaborations is that they can take us on unplanned adventures that prove life-changing. Change, however, requires openness to change. It remains to be seen whether the climate crisis will spark positive changes in our relation to the natural world.

"For as long as we continue to emit greenhouse gases, temperatures will continue to rise," says the head of the World Meteorological Organization. "Alongside that," Petteri Taalas continues, "our oceans will continue to become warmer and more acidic, sea ice and glaciers will continue to melt, sea level will continue to rise and our weather will become more extreme."[2] It is so hot in Mexico in 2024 that howler monkeys are falling out of the trees, "like apples."[3] Not our problem? Howler monkeys are warm-blooded primates about the size of a two-year-old child and a "sentinel" species, like canaries in the coal mine. Their fate warns us about our fate. Climate change remains an all-too-familiar story today as it threatens to swallow up island nations and to swamp coastal cities. Killer storms and fast-moving wildfires erase entire communities overnight. No park can offer an escape from global climate change, not even ten thousand new parks. Meanwhile, evidence mounts that the current climate change is damaging not only natural systems but also human health.[4] It is as if howler monkeys were hurling themselves out of the trees to warn us about our cholesterol levels.

"The construction of the Park," a committee report begins as early as 1868, "has been easily achieved because the industrious population of New York has been wise enough to require it, and rich enough to pay for it."[5] Human values must play a crucial role in meliorating the human-created dilemma and self-inflicted damage associated with global climate change, and urban parks can have a positive but likely modest role, no matter how many parks or how large they are. The committee report in 1868 emphasizes implied values associated with wealth, industry, and foresight, even if it also slips into self-satisfaction. It thus offers a fascinating contrast when compared with a letter to the board, dated February 1872, from the consulting landscape firm of Olmsted, Vaux & Company. Reviewing recent changes in maintenance of the park, the review even-handedly describes the differences it sees between two contrasting styles of landscape design: a European style that aims for "splendid urbanity" versus a picturesque "natural" school. The question that the firm poses, surprisingly, does not focus on aesthetic values or aesthetic taste—"Which do you like best?" "Which is most to your taste?" "Which is the latest fashion?"—but rather shifts the focus entirely to broader ethical values: "which, in this or that particular case, promises to provide most toward the fullness of life."[6]

The fullness of life is a concept that Olmsted and Vaux do not explain, but it is fundamental, if implicit, in their thinking about Central Park. "The primary purpose of the Park," Olmsted writes in 1859, "is to provide the best practicable means of healthful recreation for the inhabitants of the city, of all classes." This is not an isolated statement. "The Park," he emphasizes, "is intended to furnish healthful recreation for the poor and the rich, the young and the old, the vicious and the virtuous."[7] Health entails a broad notion of human well-being, not simply the absence of disease, and it is so important to Olmsted that he even welcomes visitors given over to vice. He also installs "keepers," of course, to assure that no one, virtuous or vicious, infringes "on the rights of others." Ethics, values, and a broad conception of human well-being, then, are basic to the creation of Central Park, and a narrow focus on landscape design neglects the underlying, basic purpose that matters most to Olmsted and Vaux: equal access to *the fullness of life*.

The close relationship between urban greenspace and human health is measurable in studies gauging the environmental impact of urban parks.[8] In replacing fetid, disease-breeding swampland with a clear pond, a wide lake, and a large new reservoir of pure drinking water, the Greensward plan makes immediate improvements in the health of New Yorkers, but the benefit continues. Trees provide a clearly measurable impact in addition to lowering temperatures in summer, reducing air pollution, and moderating ultraviolet radiation.[9] One mature tree absorbs almost fifty pounds of carbon dioxide annually. With some eighteen thousand trees today, Central Park thus sequesters an annual total of 900,000 pounds of carbon dioxide.[10] (Ten thousand Central Parks would annually trap 4.5 million tons.) The water vapor that trees release not only cools the air. High temperatures contribute to deaths from cardiovascular disease, including heart attacks and strokes, and heat-related illnesses from cramps to exhaustion are also measurably reduced in areas adjacent to urban parks. Heat-related illnesses, moreover, disproportionately strain high-risk populations. Trees even alter local wind patterns and mitigate anomalies of rain and snow.[11] The well-known value to human health from walking, exercise, and social interaction adds another indirect benefit of natural parkland, including a reduction of stress and its related maladies.

Not all such maladies are a direct result of climate change, of course, but they bear an invisible signature of the high-stress, high-tech, mechanized world that has brought us climate change. Olmsted describes a doctor who recommends that his patients take "a ride in the Park before going to their offices, and again a drive with their families before dinner."[12]

One cost-benefit analysis shows that the environmental value of planting trees exceeds the expense of maintaining them by one thousandfold.[13] Among the measurable, cost-effective benefits to health, green spaces counter social isolation, enhance relaxation, promote resilience, and improve concentration in children with attention deficit disorder.[14] Cities with the highest-ranked park systems boast residents who are 9 percent less likely to suffer from poor mental health and 21 percent less likely to be physically inactive than in other cities—the patterns intact after controlling for income, age, population density, and race or ethnicity.[15] Climate change and steady warming trends increase the well-known "heat island effect," in which urban roads and buildings cause summer temperatures to rise.[16] Urban parks in meliorating the heat island effects significantly improve various quality-of-life measures—which come about as close as statistics allow to fleshing out something of what Olmsted means by the concept of the fullness of life.

Fullness of life as inseparable from human health in the mid-nineteenth century receives its crowning emblem with the installation of Emma Stebbins's *Angel of the Waters*. The massive sculpture, raised against the sky and framed by the surrounding foliage, still occupies the place of honor it has held since 1873 atop a large fountain adjacent to the Lake. Filmmakers and amateur photographers alike seem to regard it as an iconic signature of Central Park, but many, I suspect, miss the triple allusion that Stebbins embedded in her work. The *Angel* alludes, in general, to the traditional healing properties of water, but the allusion also refers to a specific biblical episode that takes place in Jerusalem at a spa-like pool where people come in search of health: "For an angel went down at a certain season into the pool, and troubled [or stirred up] the water: whosoever then first after the troubling of the water stepped in was made whole of whatsoever disease he had" (John 5:4).

Health is the outcome associated with this angel-troubled pool, called Bethesda, and it is Stebbins's *Angel* that gives its lakeside location the name Bethesda Terrace, adopted only following the dedication of her sculpture. The third and final level of allusion, however, is historical rather than biblical or traditional. Stebbins's *Angel of the Waters*, that is, also honors the pure water transported to New York City by the Croton Aqueduct and stored in the Old Reservoir. The aqueduct is a direct response to the cholera epidemic of 1832, which kills 3,500 New Yorkers, or 1.5 percent of the population. Subsequent periodic outbreaks of cholera add a fatal disease to the hardships of life in New York City. It can kill within hours. Although its immediate cause is an aquatic bacterium, *Vibrio cholerae*, cholera is also considered a disease of poverty, primarily afflicting people who live in unsanitary conditions, including the lack of safe drinking water. It remains a killer today in parts of the world where climate change, among other related sources of social disruption, denies people access to clean water. The World Health Organization estimates that there are 1.3 to 4.0 million cases of cholera worldwide each year, with between 21,000 to 143,000 deaths.[17]

Central Park in its contributions to the fullness of life offers a response to the unhealthy, unsanitary conditions that made New York City a killing field for the immigrant population that doubles between 1850 and 1880. The city sees major outbreaks of cholera in 1849 and 1866. The blue death, as it is called, does not resemble the peaceful exits of contemporary sentimental novels. Vomiting and diarrhea drain the body of fluids and dry out the skin, imparting a bluish tint. The Council of Hygiene and Public

Bethesda Fountain & *Angel of the Waters*. Marco Rubino Photography/Alamy Stock Photo.

Health in 1867 counts fifteen thousand tenement houses in New York City, many dirt-cheap. Raw sewage seeps into the streets. It is only in the 1880s that Robert Koch identifies the culprit bacterium, and effective vaccines appear only in the 1890s. Meanwhile, cholera remains a regular summer concern. At Tosomock Farm in 1849, John worries that an outbreak will leave Frederick with three acres of unsold turnips and 35,000 unsold cabbages.[18] On September 29, 1849, the *New-York Daily Tribune* publishes a front-page chart tracking the deaths that summer in New York City from cholera, the same summer when its distinguished editor Horace Greeley loses his five-year-old son Arthur to the disease. The child's illness begins at 1:00 a.m., and by 5:00 p.m. he is dead.[19] Frederick and Mary in 1861 lose their infant son to suspected "childhood cholera."

Stebbins at the dedication ceremony admits that the sick and disabled in New York City can't expect visitation by an angel, but she adds, "we have no less healing, comfort and purification, freely sent to us through the blessed gift of pure, wholesome water, which to all the countless homes of this great city, comes like an angel visitant."[20] Today less than 1 percent of the water on Earth is drinkable freshwater, and in 2022 an outbreak of cholera in Malawi kills over one thousand villagers.[21] The blue death threatens to reemerge wherever floods, droughts, and civil conflicts force communities to live in unsanitary conditions. The threat is serious enough that global health agencies now must ration the supply of cholera vaccine.[22] Meanwhile, in an overheating world, water provides a nursery for other heat-tolerant pathogens.[23] Humans, like all animals, depend on water to avoid organ failure and death, but its blessings can slip away. The *Angel of the Waters* during the 1970s presides over a vandalized terrace, standing atop a dried-up fountain.

▰▰▰

"Climate change is primarily a water crisis," according to the United Nations.[24] In an age of melting glaciers and thawing permafrost, the *Angel of the Waters* presides over new waterborne threats to human health. Malarial mosquitos that breed in stagnant water are recolonizing areas where malaria was once expelled or controlled.[25] Aquatic frogs may be our newest sentinel. Some 90 percent of water-dependent amphibian species have gone extinct from a fungal disease that causes the skin to fall off, and climate change is partly responsible.[26] "We feel its impacts through worsening floods, rising sea levels, shrinking ice fields, wildfires and droughts," the UN warns, as even drought and wildfires reflect the lack of moisture. "Sustainable water management," it concludes, "is central to building the resilience of societies and ecosystems and to reducing carbon emissions."[27] Everything withers if plants lack the water required for photosynthesis. Less water means less food. The global demand for fresh water will outstrip supply by 40 percent within a decade, according to UN reports. Too much water is as bad as too little. Floods have left twenty million people in Pakistan in need of humanitarian aid, while a forty-year drought in Africa threatens 150 million people with famine.[28] Central Park and the *Angel of the Waters* have much to tell us about the fullness of life—and about its absences.

Peace is as basic to the fullness of life as clean drinking water, and parks at their best seem to embody peace as a fundamental value. Although Central Park can't prove to be conflict-free, I find it a remarkably peaceful place. Visitors seem to accept nonaggression and coexistence as unspoken rules of admission, which no doubt reinforces my sense of entering into a sanctuary. Other parks too seem to share this quality of peacefulness. Nelson Mandela, cofounder of the Peace Parks Foundation, saw the creation of vast parkland spaces in Africa as preventing conflict among neighboring countries and encouraging cooperation. Today the Great Limpopo Transfrontier Park links national parks in Mozambique, South Africa, and Zimbabwe, while in Mozambique the restored Gorongosa National Park provides a model for parks as providing employment for people who live nearby. "In a world beset by conflict and division," as Mandela put it, "peace is one of the cornerstones of the future. Peace parks are building blocks in this process, not only in our region, but potentially the entire world."[29] Fullness of life is an impossible dream where lives are cut short by war, famine, and disease.

Climate change cannot be dissociated from its damage to human health, which is especially why, in our own self-interest, we need hopeful action. Human-induced warming over the decade from 2014 to 2023 has been increasing at a rate that is "unprecedented in the instrumental record."[30] Proportionately increased and unprecedented action is the only sensible response, and, happily, there are hopeful signs. The Central Park Conservancy, for example, has recently partnered with Yale University to create the Central Park Climate Lab.[31] Climate change damages urban parks as well as coral reefs, and the Central Park Climate Lab aims both to measure the damage and to experiment with possible remedies, offering a model for other urban parks. This is a very small step, but a step forward, and there are an increasing number of such small steps worldwide that offer modest reason to hope.

Singapore, among the world's greenest cities, now boasts seven million trees, with one million more expected to be planted by 2030. It also maintains a digital inventory of its canopy employing laser measurements and artificial intelligence, so that arborists can monitor the health of every tree, down to its chlorophyll levels. The Singapore system is modeled on the MillionTreesNYC initiative, launched in 2007 in conjunction with a new cost-benefit software program, which has issued so far in the planting of more than a million new trees: 285,000 in Queens, 280,00 in the Bronx, 185,000 in Brooklyn, 175,000 in Staten Island, and 75,000 in Manhattan, where Central Park already supplies a significant urban woodland. Ecological engineer Nadina Galle in *The Nature of Our Cities* (2024) provides a vivid account of Fiona Watt, a parks department employee and recent forestry graduate, who is a moving force behind this particularly compelling instance of urban reforestation.[32] One dollar spent planting trees and maintaining them, as the software shows, generates $5.60 in benefits: capturing carbon dioxide, reducing energy use, decreasing air pollutants, and providing stormwater retention. Pragmatists might note that trees and urban parks help to increase local property values and to support local tax revenues.

Not everybody loves Central Park when a sudden thunderstorm sweeps through and scatters concertgoers. Forty-two million visitors each year, however, offer a good sample size, and the affection for Central Park isn't irrelevant or inconsequential. Eros raises serious ethical questions about desire; Plato makes eros his entire subject in the *Symposium*. Cultures marked by acrimonious conflict and division (call it anti-eros) might want to encourage the creation of parks that millions of people love. No sane person—I exclude developers—wants to see Central Park replaced by high-rise shopping malls, movie theaters, hotels, casinos, and apartment buildings. Simply by virtue of its vastness and the affection it inspires, Central Park demonstrates the value of engaging desires and thinking big. It is time to scale up. Why not, say, ten thousand new parks? Central Park shows that the desire for urban greenspace can move enough cartloads of topsoil to almost encircle the earth. Who, if we look at the flipside of desire, would want the people they love to experience anything less than the fullness of life?

The Earth, as scientists warned in 2023, is on the verge of "five catastrophic climate tipping points."[33] The art of the right moment has never been more consequential, since the danger is worldwide, and we may miss our last shot if opportunity passes us by. There is no guarantee of success. Hope is not about guarantees but about what we do in the extended instances when we face uncertainties, dangers, and even death. Failure is the only outcome guaranteed if we do not act. Ten thousand new people's parks, it is worth repeating, won't solve a climate crisis with five interlocked tipping points: nothing alone will solve it. Effective action, however, must embody thinking big. It must capture the imagination and engage our desires. Global climate change is a dilemma that nations must address together in a spirit of innovative collaborations. The choice to avoid collective suicide is still available, but there is no time to dither. Our actions, as ancestors, will determine the future that our grandchildren and great-grandchildren will inherit. What to do?

###

"Becoming a good ancestor," writes social philosopher Roman Krznaric, "is a formidable task."[34] Long-term thinking, in his view, is necessary for significant change. Thinking long-term is an intrinsic part of thinking big. Rajiv Shah, president of the Rockefeller Foundation, writes about very ambitious and risky projects—he calls them "big bets"—that have truly made a difference in the lives of ordinary people.[35] It is not philanthropists, organizers, policymakers, and politicians, however, who will define the future, despite their importance in shaping its directions. Shah and Krznaric emphasize as indispensable imperatives both thinking big and thinking long-term. Central Park is a symbol of the long-term benefits that flow from thinking big, taking risks, and seizing opportunities.

There is much to learn from Olmsted, Vaux, and the origins of Central Park. It is inconceivable, for example, that effectively addressing climate change won't require the exercise of eminent domain, or some equivalent legal action, to purchase land and remove homes, especially in areas prone to flood or fire. Such land might provide ideal sites for new parks that benefit the public good. It is important, however, to honor what we cannot save in the drive for renewal. The appropriate refrain for all involved might well be "Remember Seneca Village."

Skeptics can always launch reasonable objections to any risky undertaking. Climate deniers will claim that global temperatures always rise and fall, which is true but misleading. We live in a changed world. Today the world's largest institutional consumer of oil and a principal producer of greenhouse gases is the US Department of Defense.[36] It is unreasonable to abolish national defense, but it is not irrational to offer the people a tangible benefit and personal stake in parks and in urban greenspace. A carbon-capture facility in a remote location, while helpful, hardly fires the public imagination or stokes a personal desire for change. A culture in which drones or robots deliver pet food to the doorsteps of first-world consumers, while apparently reasonable, might also find the resources to promote a park-centered movement addressed to the genuine hope that we can meliorate the global climate with people-centered changes that directly serve life.

Hope in an emergency, as writer and activist Rebecca Solnit puts it, is like "an ax you break down doors with."[37] Hope serves as a tool for survival in times of crisis when we don't have the leisure for pilot studies, political gamesmanship, or running out the clock. What we need, instead of temperamental optimism or wishful thinking, is what philosopher Jonathan Lear calls *radical hope*. Radical hope is not a feeling but a moral virtue. It is an ethical stance in which individuals amid overwhelming disaster embody the courage to change.[38] Plenty Coups, the last great chief of the Crow nation, is Lear's exemplar of radical hope, responding to genocidal assaults on his people with the courage to create a new order. Central Park can offer radical hope as we face the threats of climate change and its effects in flooded cities, firestorms, broken ecosystems, vanished species, and depleted global biodiversity. Even a parable can provide an incentive for hope and change. The Good Samaritan, for example, does not just lend a hand to an unknown man left half-dead on the roadside, robbed, beaten, and stripped naked. Jews and Samaritans were enemies. The Good Samaritan rescues an enemy—an enemy whom two Jewish priests had already passed by. He cares for the man's wounds, transports him to a nearby inn, and pays the innkeeper to extend the care. A true neighbor, the parable implies, is not a person who lives next door or even a fellow worshipper, but rather someone who feels compassion and acts rightly. The parable in fact concludes (Luke 10:37) with an open call to action: "Go hence and do likewise."

Radical hope is not about wishing for help against all odds but about how we *feel* and what we *do*. It is ethical in keeping the focus on action undertaken to help others in the face of disaster.

Biologist Edward O. Wilson, a two-time winner of the Pulitzer Prize, was a distinguished scientific advocate for thinking big. In *Half-Earth: Our Planet's Fight for Life* (2016) he carefully lays the scientific groundwork for a proposal so bold that it makes ten thousand central parks seem modest: "a global network of inviolable reserves that cover half the surface of the Earth."[39] Wilson as an ardent defender of biodiversity emphasizes a need for wilderness areas: "inviolate reserves" or "wildlands," as he calls them. His overriding concern for biodiversity leads him to discredit what he calls an "Anthropocene philosophy" that in his view narrowly focuses on human needs, as distinct from the needs of the biosphere. My radical hope is that a focus on the human need for healthy parks will ultimately help repair the biosphere. I'd prefer to pursue both needs together. Parks serve human purposes that differ from the contribution of wilderness and wetlands, but the values are not intrinsically opposed. Urban parks address the inescapable fact that most people today live in cities, and the percentage is projected to rise sharply. Parks are not where we went wrong. The year 2024 included the hottest day ever recorded on the planet, July 22.[40] So far. Urban parks, with Central Park as their prototype, are where, without knowing exactly why or how, we started to go right.

Americans spend 87 percent of our lives indoors and another 6 percent in an enclosed vehicle.[41] Olmsted's founding principle that parks provide an "escape from buildings" makes increasing sense today, and the need for vast new urban parks—ten thousand is just a metaphor—may be far more urgent than skeptics imagine. Pioneers such as the New York Restoration Project are already creating small pocket parks, green spaces, and gardens, intended especially to help underserved communities.[42] Climate change, however, is so closely linked with multiple sources of environmental peril that new parks will constitute only one piece in an incomplete mosaic of mutually supporting measures. Still, they are a crucial piece. Urban parks encourage active lifestyles and reduce health costs. They cut crime, strengthen local economies, create jobs, clean the air, filter rain, reduce water pollution, manage stormwater, and mitigate floods. They even help promote the equality of conditions that Tocqueville found remarkable in American life.[43]

We know that urban parks make a positive contribution to modern life, so a bonanza of new city parkland is far from an idle pipe dream. It will take unusual collaborations, big thinking, risk-taking, and opportunities seized. This is the right moment. "If you have built castles in the air," writes Thoreau, "your work need not be lost; that is where they should be. Now put the foundations under them."[44]

NOTES

Introduction: Why Central Park?

1. United States Census Bureau, "QuickFacts Altadena CDP, California," https://www.census.gov/quickfacts/fact/table/altadenacdpcalifornia/PST045224.

2. Juanje Gómez, Andrea Fuller, Kate King, and Sarah Krouse, "$300 Million Turned to Ash: See How These Malibu Beach Homes Were Wiped Out," *Wall Street Journal*, January 18, 2025.

3. Josh Haskell, "Hundreds of Abandoned Cars on Sunset Blvd. Pushed aside by Fire Dozer," *ABC 7 Eyewitness News*, January 10, 2025; Madisen Keavy and Dean Fioresi, "Droves of Abandoned Cars Line Streets of Pacific Palisades," *KCAL News*, January 10, 2025.

4. E. O. Wilson, *Half-Earth: Our Planet's Fight for Life* (New York: Norton, 2016), 1.

5. Joan Didion, *We Tell Ourselves Stories in Order to Live: Collected Nonfiction* (New York: Knopf, 2006).

6. Friedrich Nietzsche, "On the Uses and Disadvantages of History for Life" (1874), in *Untimely Meditations*, ed. Daniel Breazeale, trans. R. J. Hollingdale (Cambridge: Cambridge University Press, 1997), 59. Nietzsche's distinctive understanding of nihilism is a complex topic. See *Nietzsche, Nihilism and the Philosophy of the Future*, ed. Jeffrey Metzger (London: Bloomsbury Academic, 2013).

7. The number, reliable as of July 2024, comes from the website of the Central Park Conservancy: https://www.centralparknyc.org/about.

8. Rais Esat, "Death Toll for Birds Hitting Buildings May Be over 1 Billion a Year in US—Report," *The Guardian*, August 7, 2024; Graham Readfearn, "Hottest Ocean Temperatures in 400 Years an 'Existential Threat' to the Great Barrier Reef, Researchers Find," *The Guardian*, August 7, 2024.

9. *Frederick Law Olmstead: Writings on Landscape, Culture, and Society*, ed. Charles E. Beveridge (New York: Library of America, 2015). The selections by Beveridge are invaluable.

10. Franz Kafka, "On Parables," in *Parables and Paradoxes* (New York: Schocken Books,

1961), 11. Kafka's term *Unfassbare*, from *fassen* (to grasp), is better translated as "ungraspable," not, as in the parallel English translation in the Schocken Books text, "incomprehensible."

11. Frederick Law Olmsted to Sylvester Baxter, November 9, 1880, in *The Papers of Frederick Law Olmsted*, ed. Charles E. Beveridge (Charlottesville: University of Virginia Press, 2022), 7:511.

1. Once Upon a Time in 1857

1. See Laura Wood Roper, *FLO: A Biography of Frederick Law Olmsted* (Baltimore: Johns Hopkins University Press, 1973), 104–6.

2. Frederick Law Olmsted to Frederick Kingsbury, November 17, 1848, in *The Papers of Frederick Law Olmsted*, ed. Charles E. Beveridge (Charlottesville: University of Virginia Press, 2022), 1:322. For clarity, I have replaced Olmsted's quotation marks with italics.

3. Roy Rosenzweig and Elizabeth Blackmar, *The Park and the People: A History of Central Park* (Ithaca, NY: Cornell University Press, 1992), 80. I am throughout deeply indebted to this brilliant and groundbreaking book.

4. Patrick Greenfield and Max Benato, "Animal Populations Experience Average Decline of Almost 70% since 1970, Report Reveals," *The Guardian*, October 12, 2022.

5. Calvert Vaux to Frederick Law Olmsted, January 18, 1864, quoted in Francis R. Kowsky, *Country, Park, & City: The Architecture and Life of Calvert Vaux* (New York: Oxford University Press, 1998), 4.

6. Rosenzweig and Blackmar, *The Park and the People*, 122.

7. Walt Whitman, *Leaves of Grass: 150th Anniversary Edition*, ed. David S. Reynolds (New York: Oxford University Press, 2005), 17.

8. Fredrika Bremer, *The Homes of the New World: Impressions of America*, trans. Mary Howitt, 2 vols. (New York: Harper & Bros., 1853), 1:46. For this and the following reference, I am indebted to Caren Yglesias, *The Complete House and Grounds: Learning from Andrew Jackson Downing's Domestic Architecture* (Chicago: Center for American Places at Columbia College Chicago, 2011), 5.

9. Frederick Law Olmsted, *The Spoils of the Park: With a Few Leaves from the Deep-Laden Note-Books of "A Wholly Unpractical Man"* (Detroit, MI: n.p., 1882), 38. The pamphlet is dated February 30, 1882.

10. Yglesias, *The Complete House and Grounds*, 5.

11. For a fine account to which I am indebted, see Francis R. Kowsky, "The Dual Career of Calvert Vaux, Architect and Landscape Architect," *Olmsted Network*, July 2, 2024, https://olmsted.org/the-dual-career-of-calvert-vaux-architect-and-landscape-architect.

12. Andrew Jackson Downing, "The New-York Park," *The Horticulturist* 6, no. 8 (August 1851): 345; "Mr. Downing's Letters from England," 153.

2. Olmsted Seeking Olmsted

1. Addy Bink and Nexstar Media Wire, "Mega Millions: Are Your Jackpot Odds Worse When More People Play?," *The Hill*, January 6, 2023.

2. Frederick Law Olmsted to Elizabeth Baldwin Whitney, December 16, 1890, in *The Papers of Frederick Law Olmsted*, ed. Charles E. Beveridge (Charlottesville: University of Virginia Press, 2022), 9:247. Subsequent citations are abbreviated *PFLO*.

3. Ibid.

4. Walt Whitman, as recounted by author John Townsend Trowbridge. Quoted in David S. Reynolds, *Walt Whitman's America: A Cultural Biography* (New York: Vintage Books, 1995), 82.

5. Ralph Waldo Emerson, "Self-Reliance" (1841), in *Essays & Lectures*, ed. Joel Porte (New York: Library of America, 1983), 275.

6. See Justin Martin, "Olmsted's Staten Island Farm," Cultural Landscape Foundation, July 3, 2019, https://www.tclf.org/olmsted-staten-island-farm.

7. Frederick Law Olmsted, *Public Parks and the Enlargement of Towns* (1870; repr., New York: Arno Press, 1970), 34. The essay was first read before the American Social Science Association at the Lowell Institute, Boston, and soon published as a pamphlet.

8. Charles Capen McLaughlin, "Frederick Law Olmsted: His Life and Work," *PFLO* 1:7.

9. "Frederick Law Olmsted Finds a Wife (But It Wasn't Easy)," New England Historical Society, updated 2022, https://newenglandhistoricalsociety.com/frederick-law-olmsted-finds -wife/.

10. McLaughlin, "Frederick Law Olmsted," *PFLO* 1:11.

11. Emerson, "Self-Reliance," 277–78.

12. Frederick Law Olmsted, *Walks and Talks of an American Farmer in England* (1852; repr., Amherst: University of Massachusetts Press, 2002), 91; punctuation normalized.

13. Ralph Waldo Emerson, "Fate," in *Essays & Lectures*, 966.

14. Walt Whitman, "Song of Myself" (1855), in *Leaves of Grass*, Walt Whitman Archive, https://whitmanarchive.org.

3. Paperback Writer

1. For early American printing practices, see James N. Green, "Bound/Unbound," *Early American Studies* 16, no. 4 (2018): 614–20.

2. Jill Lepore, *The Story of America: Essays on Origins* (Princeton, NJ: Princeton University Press, 2012), 212–14; Bill Brown, ed., *Reading the West: An Anthology of Dime Novels* (Boston: Bedford, 1997).

3. Fredrika Bremer, *The Homes of the New World: Impressions of America*, trans. Mary Howitt, 2 vols. (New York: Harper & Bros., 1853), 1:46; italics substituted for clarity.

4. Rebecca Solnit, *Hope in the Dark: Untold Histories, Wild Possibilities* (2004), 3rd ed. (Chicago: Haymarket Books, 2016), 60, 66.

5. The three travel books are *A Journey in the Seaboard Slave States* (1856), *A Journey through Texas* (1857), and *A Journey in the Back Country* (1860). The compilation—usually abbreviated as *The Cotton Kingdom*—is titled *The Cotton Kingdom: A Traveller's Observations on Cotton and Slavery in the American Slave States. Based upon Three Former Volumes of Journeys and Investigations* (1861).

6. Walt Whitman, *Leaves of Grass: 150th Anniversary Edition*, ed. David S. Reynolds (New York: Oxford University Press, 2005), 40.

7. Wayfarer [Frederick Law Olmsted], "The People's Park at Birkenhead, Near Liverpool," *The Horticulturist* 6, no. 5 (May 1851): 224–28; Anon., review of *Walks and Talks of an American Farmer in England*, by F. L. Olmsted, *The Horticulturist* 8, no. 1 (January 1853): 43–46. Tellingly, the review identifies the anonymous author as Olmstead.

8. Walt Whitman, "Song of the Open Road" (1867), in *Leaves of Grass*, The Walt Whitman Archive, https://whitmanarchive.org. *Leaves of Grass* receives an enthusiastic review in *Putnam's*

Monthly in 1855, the same year when Olmsted becomes a partner in the publishing firm Dix, Edwards & Company, with editorial assignments for its journal *Putnam's Monthly*. *Leaves of Grass* undergoes numerous editions and revisions after its publication in 1855.

9. D. H. Lawrence, *Studies in Classic American Literature* (New York: Thomas Seltzer, 1923), 256, 255; for clarity, italics replace quotation marks. See also John Milton, *Paradise Lost*, ed. John Leonard (New York: Penguin Books, 2000), XII.646–47.

10. Frederick Law Olmsted, *Walks and Talks of an American Farmer in England* (1852; repr., Amherst: University of Massachusetts Press, 2002), 91.

11. Andrew Jackson Downing, "The New-York Park," *The Horticulturist* 6, no. 8 (August 1851): 348.

12. [William Cullen Bryant], "A New Public Park," *Evening Post*, July 3, 1844.

13. Downing, like some others, recommended a five-hundred-acre West Side site "between 39th-street and the Harlem River." *The Horticulturist* 6, no. 8 (August 1851): 347. An East Side riverfront locale, Jones Wood, was also often proposed as the site for a city park.

14. See Roy Rosenzweig and Elizabeth Blackmar, *The Park and the People: A History of Central Park* (Ithaca, NY: Cornell University Press, 1992).

15. Sara Cedar Miller, *Before Central Park* (New York: Columbia University Press, 2022), 172.

16. New York City Board of Aldermen, *Documents*, January 2, 1852, quoted in Rosenzweig and Blackmar, *The Park and the People*, 45.

17. Frederick Law Olmsted to Frederick Kingsbury, October 17, 1852, in *The Papers of Frederick Law Olmsted*, ed. Charles E. Beveridge (Charlottesville: University of Virginia Press, 2022), 2:82.

18. Jill Lepore, *These Truths: A History of the United States* (New York: Norton, 2018), 168, 255.

19. Quotations from Lowell and Norton are found in Laura Wood Roper, *FLO: A Biography of Frederick Law Olmsted* (Baltimore: Johns Hopkins University Press, 1973), 152.

20. Justin Martin, *Genius of Place: The Life of Frederick Law Olmsted* (New York: Da Capo Press, 2011), 125.

4. A Young Snowy Owl

1. Amitav Ghosh, *The Great Derangement: Climate Change and the Unthinkable* (Chicago: University of Chicago Press, 2016), 32.

2. Michelle Megna, "Pet Ownership Statistics 2024," *Forbes*, January 25, 2024.

3. See Edward O. Wilson, *Biophilia: The Human Bond with Other Species*, rev. ed. (Cambridge, MA: Harvard University Press, 1984); Stephen R. Kellert and Edward O. Wilson, eds., *The Biophilia Hypothesis* (Mercer Island, WA: Island Books, 1993); and Donna J. Haraway, *The Companion Species Manifesto* (Chicago: University of Chicago Press, 2003).

4. Henry D. Thoreau, *Walden* (1854), ed. Jeffrey S. Cramer (New Haven, CT: Yale University Press, 2004), 16 ("Economy").

5. See Roy Rosenzweig and Elizabeth Blackmar, *The Park and the People: A History of Central Park* (Ithaca, NY: Cornell University Press, 1992); and Sara Cedar Miller, *Before Central Park* (New York: Columbia University Press, 2022).

6. Theresa Machemer, "Snowy Owl Stops in Central Park for the First Time since 1890," *Smithsonian Magazine*, January 29, 2021.

7. Dani Anguiano, "Crowds Flock to US Suburb to Witness Snowy Owl Visiting from the Arctic," *The Guardian*, January 12, 2023.

8. Erich Fromm, *The Anatomy of Human Destructiveness* (New York: Holt, Rinehart & Winston, 1973), 406.

9. Cal Vornberger, *Birds of Central Park* (New York: Harry N. Abrams, 2005), 8.

10. Ibid., 8; Gustave Axelson, "Vanishing: More Than 1 In 4 Birds Has Disappeared in the Last 50 Years," *All About Birds*, The Cornell Lab of Ornithology, September 19, 2019, https://www.allaboutbirds.org/news/vanishing-1-in-4-birds-gone/.

11. Mark Cocker, "Look up, Listen, and Be Very Concerned. Birds Are Vanishing—and Their Crisis Is Our Crisis," *The Guardian*, April 17, 2023.

12. Ed Shanahan, "Flaco, Escaped Central Park Zoo Owl and Defier of Doubts, Is Dead," *New York Times*, February 23, 2024.

13. Lauren Evans, "Pale Male Is a Legend—But Is He Still Alive?," Audubon, June 7, 2019, https://www.audubon.org/news/pale-male-legend-he-still-alive.

14. Hannah Frishberg, "Celebrity Bald Eagle Rover Makes Triumphant Return to Central Park," *New York Post*, January 24, 2024; italics added.

15. Henry D. Thoreau, "Walking" (1862), in *Essays*, ed. Jeffrey S. Cramer (New Haven, CT: Yale University Press, 2013), 260.

16. Frederick Law Olmsted, quoted in Charles E. Beveridge, "Introduction," in *The Papers of Frederick Law Olmsted*, ed. Charles E. Beveridge (Charlottesville: University of Virginia Press, 2022), 3:15. The passage is from Olmsted's draft manuscript "Influence."

17. Rosenzweig and Blackmar, *The Park and the People*, 139.

18. Rolf Diamant, "The Olmsteds and the Development of the National Park System," Olmsted Network, July 5, 2023, https://olmsted.org/the-olmsteds-and-the-development-of-the-national-park-system/.

19. Clarence C. Cook, *A Description of the New York Central Park* (1869; repr., New York: New York University Press, 2017), 107.

20. Thoreau, "Life without Principle" (1863), in *Essays*, 351.

21. William Blake, *The Marriage of Heaven and Hell*, in *The Complete Poetry and Prose of William Blake*, ed. David V. Erdman, rev. ed. (Berkeley: University of California Press, 1982), 87 (l. 54).

22. Brooke Bateman, "False Springs: How Earlier Spring with Climate Change Wreaks Havoc on Birds," Audubon, September 25, 2020, https://www.audubon.org/news/false-springs-how-earlier-spring-climate-change-wreaks-havoc-birds.

5. An Unpractical Man

1. See Lee Hall, *Olmsted's America: An "Unpractical" Man and His Vision of Civilization* (Boston: Little, Brown and Company, 1995), 187–231.

2. Witold Rybczynski, *A Clearing in the Distance: Frederick Law Olmsted and America in the 19th Century* (New York: Scribner, 1999), 157.

3. Frederick Law Olmsted, "Passages in the Life of an Unpractical Man," in *The Papers of Frederick Law Olmsted*, ed. Charles E. Beveridge (Charlottesville: University of Virginia Press, 2022), 3:90. Subsequent citations are abbreviated *PFLO*.

4. Charles E. Beveridge, "Introduction," *PFLO* 3:17.

5. Frederick Law Olmsted, *A Journey through Texas: Or a Saddle-Trip on the Southwestern Frontier* (1857; repr., Lincoln: University of Nebraska Press, 2004), 74.

6. Frederick Law Olmsted, "Passages in the Life of an Unpractical Man," *PFLO* 3:88.

7. Frederick Law Olmsted to John Hull Olmsted, September 11, 1857, *PFLO* 3:79.

8. Rybczynski, *A Clearing in the Distance*, 156.

9. Frederick Law Olmsted, "Passages in the Life of an Unpractical Man," *PFLO* 3:89–90.

10. George Templeton Strong, *The Diary of George Templeton Strong*, ed. Allan Nevins and Milton Halsey Thomas, 4 vols. (New York: Macmillan, 1952), 3:326, quoted in Laura Wood Roper, *FLO: A Biography of Frederick Law Olmsted* (Baltimore: Johns Hopkins University Press, 1973), 219. Like Olmsted, Strong served during the Civil War with the United States Sanitary Commission.

11. Frederick Law Olmsted to John Olmsted, January 14, 1858, *PFLO* 3:113.

12. Ralph Waldo Emerson, "Culture" (1860), in *Essays & Lectures*, ed. Joel Porte (New York: Library of America, 1983), 1,019. See also Roper, *FLO*, 339–40.

13. Roper, *FLO*, 134.

14. Frederick Law Olmsted to John Olmsted, October 9, 1857, *PFLO* 3:104.

15. John Olmsted to Frederick Law Olmsted, November 28, 1857, quoted in Roper, *FLO*, 133.

16. John Hull Olmsted to Frederick Law Olmsted, November 13, 1857, quoted in Roper, *FLO*, 133.

6. Enter Calvert Vaux

1. "Landscape Architect for the Nation, 1865–1903," Frederick Law Olmsted Papers, Library of Congress, https://www.loc.gov/collections/frederick-law-olmsted-papers/articles-and-essays/timeline/landscape-architect-for-the-nation-1865-to-1903.

2. See Eric Charles White, *Kaironomia: On the Will-to-Invent* (Ithaca, NY: Cornell University Press, 1987).

3. Clarence C. Cook, *A Description of the New York Central Park* (1869; repr., New York: New York University Press, 2017), 24. For Viele's plan, see the New York Public Library Digital Collections, Image ID 1697276.

4. Frederick Law Olmsted to Mariana Griswold Van Rensselaer, May 22, 1893, in *The Papers of Frederick Law Olmsted*, ed. Charles E. Beveridge (Charlottesville: University of Virginia Press, 2022), 9:624. Subsequent citations are abbreviated *PFLO*.

5. Ibid.

6. Calvert Vaux, *Villas and Cottages*, 2nd ed. (New York: Harper and Brothers, 1864), 44.

7. Calvert Vaux to Frederick Law Olmsted, June 3, [1865], *PFLO* 3:388.

8. "How a 'Ladies Pavilion' ended up in Central Park," Ephemeral New York, June 19, 2017, https://ephemeralnewyork.wordpress.com/tag/jacob-wray-mould-central-park.

9. Francis R. Kowsky, *Country, Park, & City: The Architecture and Life of Calvert Vaux* (New York: Oxford University Press, 1998), 23; Calvert Vaux to Frederick Law Olmsted, July 31, 1865, *PFLO* 3:66.

10. Ralph Waldo Emerson, "The American Scholar" (1837), in *Essays & Lectures*, ed. Joel Porte (New York: Library of America, 1983), 70.

11. Uvedale Price, *An Essay on the Picturesque, as Compared with the Sublime and the Beautiful* (London: J. Robson, 1794), 34.

12. William Gilpin, *Three Essays: On Picturesque Beauty; On Picturesque Travel; and on Sketching Landscape* (London: R. Blamire, 1792), 42.

13. Frederick Law Olmsted to Elizabeth Baldwin Whitney, December 16, 1890, *PFLO* 9:248.

14. Frederick Law Olmsted, *Public Parks and the Enlargement of Towns* (1870; repr., New York: Arno Press, 1970), 23.

15. Calvert Vaux to Clarence C. Cook, June 6, 1865, quoted in Cynthia S. Brenwall, *The Central Park: Original Designs for New York's Greatest Treasure* (New York: Abrams, 2019), 13. My discussion of Bow Bridge is indebted to Brenwall's account.

16. "Bridge No. 28," Central Park Conservancy, https://www.centralparknyc.org/locations /bridge-no-28; "The Bridges of Central Park," NYC Parks, https://www.nycgovparks.org/parks /central-park/highlights/11983.

17. Brenwall, *The Central Park*, 51.

18. See Sara Cedar Miller, *Before Central Park* (New York: Columbia University Press, 2022), 342–43, 351–53.

19. *PFLO* 3:90n.

20. Calvert Vaux to Frederick Law Olmsted, July 31, 1865, quoted in *PFLO* 3:66.

7. The Weeping Time

1. See Anne C. Bailey, *The Weeping Time: Memory and the Largest Slave Auction in American History* (New York: Cambridge University Press, 2017).

2. "A Great Slave Auction," *New-York Daily Tribune*, March 9, 1859.

3. Frederick Law Olmsted, *A Journey through Texas: Or a Saddle-Trip on the Southwestern Frontier* (1857; repr., Lincoln: University of Nebraska Press, 2004), 105. The episode also reappears in the second volume of *The Cotton Kingdom*.

4. Roy Rosenzweig and Elizabeth Blackmar, *The Park and the People: A History of Central Park* (Ithaca, NY: Cornell University Press, 1992), 176.

5. Ibid., 150; "Introduction," *The Papers of Frederick Law Olmsted*, ed. Charles E. Beveridge (Charlottesville: University of Virginia Press, 2022), 3:18. Subsequent citations are abbreviated *PFLO*.

6. Samuel Parsons, "History of the Development of Central Park," *Proceedings of the New York State Historical Association* 17 (1919): 168.

7. Frederick Law Olmsted, "Passages in the Life of an Unpractical Man," *PFLO* 3:90.

8. Frederick Law Olmsted, *The Cotton Kingdom: A Traveller's Observations on Cotton and Slavery in the American Slave States, 1853–1861*, 2 vols., 2nd ed. (1862; repr., Ann Arbor: Michigan Historical Reprint Series, 2022), 1:198.

9. Thomas Carlyle, *Past and Present* (1843), ed. Richard D. Altick (New York: New York University Press, 1977), 202 ("Reward"). Carlyle alludes to Jesus: "We must work the works of him that sent me, while it is day: the night cometh, when no man can work" (John 9:4).

10. Frederick Law Olmsted to John Olmsted, August 12, 1846, *PFLO* 1:272.

11. Ibid.; Frederick Law Olmsted to Charles Loring Brace, March 15, 1887, *PFLO* 8:369.

12. Frederick Law Olmsted to *New-York Daily Times*, February 13, 1854, *PFLO* 2:260.

13. Ibid., *PFLO* 2:263.

14. Frederick Law Olmsted to John Bigelow, February 9, 1861, *PFLO* 3:324; Frederick Law Olmsted to Calvert Vaux, February 16, 1863, *PFLO* 7:515.

15. Frederick Law Olmsted, "Dedication," *The Cotton Kingdom*; John Stuart Mill, "The Contest in America," *Fraser's Magazine* 65, no. 386 (February 1862): 264.

16. Charles Sumner, *The Crime against Kansas* (Boston: John P. Jewett & Company, 1856), 6.

17. Laura Wood Roper, *FLO: A Biography of Frederick Law Olmsted* (Baltimore: Johns Hopkins University Press, 1973), 134.

18. Samuel Longfellow, ed., *Life of Henry Wadsworth Longfellow: With Extracts From His Journals and Correspondence*, 2 vols. (Boston: Ticknor and Company, 1886), 2:361;

capitalization normalized. I owe this quotation, as well as reference to protests by the wives and widows of Confederate soldiers, to Jill Lepore, *These Truths: A History of the United States* (New York: Norton, 2018), 290, 302.

8. The Greensward Plan

1. Roy Rosenzweig and Elizabeth Blackmar, *The Park and the People: A History of Central Park* (Ithaca, NY: Cornell University Press, 1992), 119.

2. See Cynthia S. Brenwall, *The Central Park: Original Designs for New York's Greatest Treasure* (New York: Abrams, 2019).

3. Calvert Vaux to Frederick Law Olmsted, June 3, 1865, in *The Papers of Frederick Law Olmsted*, ed. Charles E. Beveridge (Charlottesville: University of Virginia Press, 2022), 3:269. Spelling normalized. Subsequent citations are abbreviated *PFLO*.

4. Elizabeth Barlow Rogers, *Saving Central Park: A History and a Memoir* (New York: Alfred A. Knopf, 2018), 20.

5. "The Greensward," NYC Municipal Archives, Department of Records & Information Services, April 8, 2022, https://www.archives.nyc/blog/2022/4/8/the-greensward.

6. Frederick Law Olmsted, *Walks and Talks of an American Farmer in England* (1852; repr., Amherst: University of Massachusetts Press, 2002), 91, 409. The earlier usage is hyphenated: *green-sward*.

7. Calvert Vaux to Frederick Law Olmsted, June 3, [1865], *PFLO* 5:387. Spelling normalized.

8. Ibid.

9. Calvert Vaux, *Villas and Cottages*, 2nd ed. (New York: Harper and Brothers, 1864), 51.

10. Frederick Law Olmsted, *The Spoils of the Park: With a Few Leaves from the Deep-Laden Note-Books of "A Wholly Unpractical Man"* (Detroit, MI: n.p., 1882), 35.

11. Olmsted, *Walks and Talks*, 145.

12. "Illusion lay at the heart of Greensward": Witold Rybczynski, *A Clearing in the Distance: Frederick Law Olmsted and America in the 19th Century* (New York: Scribner, 1999), 166. Rybczynski is right that everything is transformed, not what it once was, but *illusion* strikes me as a misleading term to describe the result.

13. Olmsted, *The Spoils of the Park*, 51.

14. Frederic B. Perkins and W. H. Guild, *The Central Park* (New York: n.p., 1868), 13. Guild provides the photographs.

15. Clarence C. Cook, *A Description of Central Park* (1869; rpt. New York: New York University Press, 2017), 106, 115.

16. Ibid., 116.

17. Frederick Law Olmsted to the Board of Commissioners, May 31, 1858, *PFLO* 3:196.

18. Cook, *A Description of Central Park*, 110.

19. Frederick Law Olmsted to Calvert Vaux, September 3, 1887, Calvert Vaux Papers, Manuscripts and Archives Division, New York Public Library.

20. Olmsted, *Walks and Talks*, 407.

9. The Wiping Out of Seneca Village

1. Elizabeth Kolbert, *The Sixth Extinction: An Unnatural History* (New York: Henry Holt, 2014), 17.

2. "Nature's Dangerous Decline 'Unprecedented'; Species Extinction Rates 'Accelerating,'"

UN Environment Programme, May 6, 2019, https://www.unep.org/news-and-stories/press
-release/natures-dangerous-decline-unprecedented-species-extinction-rates.

3. Roy Rosenzweig and Elizabeth Blackmar, *The Park and the People: A History of Central Park* (Ithaca, NY: Cornell University Press, 1992), 78, 81.

4. Ibid., 225, 72.

5. Frederick Law Olmsted to Frederick Kingsbury, October 17, 1852, in *The Papers of Frederick Law Olmsted*, ed. Charles E. Beveridge (Charlottesville: University of Virginia Press, 2022), 2:83. Subsequent citations are abbreviated *PFLO.*

6. Witold Rybczynski, *A Clearing in the Distance: Frederick Law Olmsted and America in the 19th Century* (New York: Scribner, 1999), 120.

7. Frederick Law Olmsted, *The Cotton Kingdom: A Traveller's Observations on Cotton and Slavery in the American Slave States, 1853–1861*, 2 vols., 2nd ed. (1862; repr., Ann Arbor: The Michigan Historical Reprint Series, 2022), 1:2.

8. Frederick Law Olmsted to John Olmsted, September 23, 1859, *PFLO* 3:230.

9. See appendix II, *PFLO* 3:454.

10. Rosenzweig and Blackmar, *The Park and the People*, 88–89.

11. Marie Warsh, "Dishes, Shoes, and Tiles: The Excavation of the Seneca Village Site," *Central Park Conservancy Magazine*, February 7, 2019; "Archaeology," Seneca Village Project, https://projects.mcah.columbia.edu/seneca_village/htm/archaeology.htm. See also Sara Cedar Miller, *Before Central Park* (New York: Columbia University Press, 2022), 172-210.

12. Olmsted, *The Cotton Kingdom*, 1:36. For clarity, quotation marks are replaced with italics.

13. *Seneca's Morals Abstracted in Three Parts*, trans. Roger L'Estrange (London, 1679), II.i ("Of a happy life"). Typography normalized.

14. See Iljoong Kim, Hojun Lee, and Ilya Somin, eds., *Eminent Domain: A Comparative Perspective* (Cambridge: Cambridge University Press, 2017).

15. Miller, *Before Central Park*, 363.

16. Ibid., 358. For an account of land values in Seneca Village, see 361–64.

17. Mindy Thompson Fullilove, *Eminent Domain and African Americans: What Is the Price of the Commons?*, vol. 1, Perspectives on Eminent Domain Abuse (Institute for Justice, February 2007), https://ij.org/report/eminent-domain-african-americans/.

18. Frederick Law Olmsted to Elizabeth Baldwin Whitney, December 16, 1890, *PFLO* 9:246.

19. Ibid.

20. Frederick Law Olmsted to John Olmsted, October 21, 1860, *PFLO* 3:275.

21. Personal column, *National Anti-Slavery Standard*, August 11, 1860; punctuation slightly altered.

22. Ibid., August 25, 1860.

23. Rosenzweig and Blackmar, *The Park and the People*, 191.

24. Frederick Law Olmsted to John Olmsted, October 21, 1860, *PFLO* 3:275.

25. Frederick Law Olmsted to John Olmsted, November 15, 1860, quoted in Laura Wood Roper, *FLO: A Biography of Frederick Law Olmsted* (Baltimore: Johns Hopkins University Press, 1973), 151.

10. An Escape from Buildings

1. Frederick Law Olmsted, *The Spoils of the Park: With a Few Leaves from the Deep-Laden Note-Books of "A Wholly Unpractical Man"* (Detroit, MI: n.p., 1882), 6.

2. Frederick Law Olmsted to John Olmsted, September 23, 1859, in *The Papers of Frederick Law Olmsted*, ed. Charles E. Beveridge (Charlottesville: University of Virginia Press, 2022), 3:230. Subsequent citations are abbreviated *PFLO*.

3. Carol J. Nicholson, "Elegance and Grass Roots: The Neglected Philosophy of Frederick Law Olmsted," *Transactions of the Charles S. Peirce Society* 40, no. 2 (2004): 336.

4. Laura Wood Roper, *FLO: A Biography of Frederick Law Olmsted* (Baltimore: Johns Hopkins University Press, 1973), 211.

5. Olmsted, *The Spoils of the Park*, 6.

6. Frederick Wiseman, *Central Park: A Look at the Famous New York Landmark* (1990), Zipporah Films, 176 minutes.

7. Frederick Law Olmsted to Mariana Griswold Van Rensselaer, May 22, 1893, *PFLO* 9:624.

8. Olmsted, *The Spoils of the Park*, 6.

9. Frederick Law Olmsted, "Park," *PFLO* 3:354. This encyclopedia entry, written while he was at work on Central Park, appeared in the *New American Cyclopaedia* (1861).

10. Roy Rosenzweig and Elizabeth Blackmar, *The Park and the People: A History of Central Park* (Ithaca, NY: Cornell University Press, 1992), 309.

11. See Sumedha M. Joshi, "The Sick Building Syndrome," *Indian Journal of Occupational and Environmental Medicine* 12, no. 2 (2008): 61–64.

12. See Kathleen Kreiss, "Sick Building Syndrome and Building-Related Illness," in *Environmental and Occupational Medicine*, ed. William N. Rom and Steven B. Markowitz, 4th ed. (New York: Lippincott Williams & Wilkins, 2006), 1,373–80; and "Indoor Air Facts No. 4 (Revised): Sick Building Syndrome," US Environmental Protection Agency, February 1991, https://www.epa.gov/sites/default/files/2014–08/documents/sick_building _factsheet.pdf.

13. Rosenzweig and Blackmar, *The Park and the People*, 211.

14. Frederick Law Olmsted and Calvert Vaux, "Description of a Plan for the Improvement of the Central Park 'Greensward,'" *PFLO* 3:132.

15. "Description of the Central Park" (1859), *PFLO* 3:212–13.

16. Melanie Grayce West, "Alfred J. Shuman Gives $5 Million to Central Park Conservancy," *Wall Street Journal*, November 24, 2014.

17. Rosenzweig and Blackmar, *The Park and the People*, 451. I am indebted to the authors throughout and here in particular.

18. Frederick Law Olmsted, "Instructions to All Engaged in Moving or Planting Trees or Shrubs," c. June 27, 1860, *PFLO* 3:255.

19. Samuel Parsons, "History of the Development of Central Park," *Proceedings of the New York State Historical Association* 17 (1919): 168. For Olmsted's estimate of nearly ten million "one-horse cart-loads," see Beveridge, "Introduction," *PFLO* 3:17.

20. Calvert Vaux, [March 1864], quoted in *PFLO* 3:185n23. For clarity, "ramble" is capitalized.

21. Olmsted, *The Spoils of the Park*, 36.

22. Doris Lessing, "The Art of Fiction CII," interview by Thomas Frick, *Paris Review* 106 (Spring 1988): 90.

23. The phrase comes from M. M. Bakhtin, "Epic and Novel: Towards a Methodology for the Study of the Novel" (1970), in *The Dialogic Imagination: Four Essays by M. M. Bakhtin*, trans. and ed. Michael Holquist and Caryl Emerson (Austin: University of Texas Press, 1981). The essay first appeared in 1941 under a different title ("The Novel as a Literary Genre").

24. The Doomsday Clock is based on estimates regarding nuclear risk, climate change, and disruptive technologies. See https://thebulletin.org/doomsday-clock/.

11. Sideways Time Travel

1. Frederick Law Olmsted to the Board of Commissioners, January 22, 1861, in *The Papers of Frederick Law Olmsted*, ed. Charles E. Beveridge (Charlottesville: University of Virginia Press, 2022), 3:304. Subsequent citations are abbreviated *PFLO*. Punctuation normalized.

2. Walt Whitman, "Central Park Walks and Talks," *Specimen Days* (1882), Whitman Archive, https://whitmanarchive.org/item/ppp.00504#leaf070v1. The piece was first published in *the New York Tribune* on May 24, 1879, and the title "Walks and Talks" is likely an homage to Olmsted's *Walks and Talks of an American Farmer in England*.

3. Bernard Weinraub, "10,000 Chant 'L-O-V-E,'" *New York Times*, March 27, 1967.

4. Ibid.

5. Frederick Law Olmsted to Elizabeth Baldwin Whitney, December 16, 1890, *PFLO* 9:246. He had written earlier: "I begin to think I *do* love Miss B. Really. The fact is—never mind. If I never did before I do now. What a blessed thing she must be" (Olmstead to Charles Loring Brace, March 27, 1846, *PFLO* 1:234).

6. See Maurice Isserman, "My First Antiwar Protest," *New York Times*, April 14, 2017.

7. Lacey Fosburgh, "Thousands of Homosexuals Hold a Protest Rally in Central Park," *New York Times*, June 29, 1970. The *Times* briefly mentions the raid on the Stonewall Inn but does not explicitly connect the protest to its anniversary, and the headline term "homosexuals" reflects a larger moment on the cusp of change.

8. Press Release, "Cleopatra's Needle," Metropolitan Museum of Art, November 20, 2013, https://www.metmuseum.org/press/exhibitions/2013/cleopatras-needle.

9. See Mark Bulik, *Ambush at Central Park: When the IRA Came to New York* (New York: Fordham University Press, 2023).

10. Associated Press in New York, "Central Park Five's Yusef Salaam Wins Democratic City Council Primary," *The Guardian*, July 5, 2023.

11. Mary Walrath-Holdridge, "Yusef Salaam, Member of the Central Park Five, Runs for New York City Office," *USA Today*, June 22, 2023.

12. Sarah Maslin Nir, "How 2 Lives Collided in Central Park, Rattling the Nation," *New York Times*, updated October 14, 2020; Jan Ransom, "Amy Cooper Faces Charges After Calling Police on Black Bird-Watcher," *New York Times*, updated October 14, 2020.

13. William Zorach, *Art Is My Life: The Autobiography of William Zorach* (New York: World Publishing, 1967), 23, 34, 37.

14. Clarence C. Cook, *A Description of the New York Central Park* (1869; repr., New York: New York University Press, 2017), 81, 74–75.

15. Eliza Shapiro, "$160 Million Later, New Pool and Rink Will Replace Central Park Eyesore," *New York Times*, October 9, 2024.

16. Oliver Milman and Aliya Uteuova, "Parts of US See Earliest Spring Conditions on Record: 'Climate Change Playing out in Real Time,'" *The Guardian*, February 24, 2023; Mike Lockwood et al., "Frost Fairs, Sunspots and the Little Ice Age," *Astronomy & Geophysics* 58, no. 2 (2017): 2.17–23.

12. A People's Park

1. Alexis de Tocqueville, *Democracy in America* (1835/1840), trans. and ed. Harvey C. Mansfield and Delba Winthrop (Chicago: University of Chicago Press, 2000), 3. On Olmsted's

reading of Tocqueville, see Laura Wood Roper, *FLO: A Biography of Frederick Law Olmsted* (Baltimore: Johns Hopkins University Press, 1973), 247.

2. Tocqueville, *Democracy in America*, 326.

3. Calvert Vaux, *Villas and Cottages*, 2nd ed. (New York: Harper and Brothers, 1864), 50.

4. Frederick Law Olmsted, *Walks and Talks of an American Farmer in England* (1852; repr., Amherst: University of Massachusetts Press, 2002), 92, 93.

5. Luna Shyr, "Portals in Time: The Story of Central Park's Named Gates," *Central Park Conservancy Magazine*, October 4, 2022.

6. Ralph Waldo Emerson, "The American Scholar" (1837), in *Essays & Lectures*, ed. Joel Porte (New York: Library of America, 1983), 54.

7. Committee on Statuary, Fountains, and Architecture to the Board of Commissioners, April 10, 1862, quoted in Shyr, "Portals in Time."

8. Frederick Law Olmsted, *Public Parks and the Enlargement of Towns* (1870; repr., New York: Arno Press, 1970), 21–22.

9. Roy Rosenzweig and Elizabeth Blackmar, *The Park and the People: A History of Central Park* (Ithaca, NY: Cornell University Press, 1992), 213, 308, 313–14.

10. Frederick Law Olmsted to the Board of Commissioners, May 31, 1858, in *The Papers of Frederick Law Olmsted*, ed. Charles E. Beveridge (Charlottesville: University of Virginia Press, 2022), 3:196. Subsequent citations are abbreviated *PFLO*.

11. See Rosenzweig and Blackmar, *The Park and the People*, 196–99.

12. Calvert Vaux, letter to the editor, *Evening Post*, May 9, 1865; spelling normalized.

13. [Clarence C. Cook], "Mr. Hunt's Designs for the Gates of the Central Park," *New-York Daily Tribune*, August 2, 1865. See also Maureen Meister, introduction to Clarence C. Cook, *A Description of the New York Central Park* (1869; repr., New York: New York University Press, 2017), xvi.

14. Walt Whitman, *Leaves of Grass: 150th Anniversary Edition*, ed. David S. Reynolds (New York: Oxford University Press, 2005), 17.

15. Reece Nortum, "In the Limelight: A Civil War Military Innovation," Hampton Roads Naval Museum, September 30, 2016.

16. Cook, *A Description of Central Park*, 64.

17. *New York Herald*, December 17, 1858, quoted in Justin Martin, *Genius of Place: The Life of Frederick Law Olmsted* (New York: Da Capo Press, 2011), 153.

18. Walt Whitman, "A Fine Afternoon, 4 to 6," *Specimen Days* (1882), Whitman Archive, https://whitmanarchive.org/item/ppp.00504#leaf070v. The piece first appeared in the *New York Tribune*, May 24, 1879.

19. Calvert Vaux to Frederick Law Olmsted, June 3, [1865], *PFLO* 5:387.

20. Tocqueville, *Democracy in America*, 47.

13. Imagination & Machinery

1. Frederick Law Olmsted to the Board of Commissioners, January 22, 1861, in *The Papers of Frederick Law Olmsted*, ed. Charles E. Beveridge (Charlottesville: University of Virginia Press, 2022), 3:319. Subsequent citations are abbreviated *PFLO*.

2. Ralph Waldo Emerson, *Nature* (1836), in *Essays & Lectures*, ed. Joel Porte (New York: Library of America, 1983), 12 ("Commodity"): Man "no longer waits for favoring gales, but by means of steam, he realizes the fable of Aeolus's bag, and carries the two and thirty winds in the boiler of his boat."

3. Henry D. Thoreau, *Walden* (1854), ed. Jeffrey S. Cramer (New Haven, CT: Yale University Press, 2004), 98–99 ("Where I Lived and What I Lived For").

4. Frederick Law Olmsted to Bertha Olmsted, January 28, 1862, *PFLO* 4:256.

5. Clarence C. Cook, *A Description of the New York Central Park* (1869; repr., New York: New York University Press, 2017), 28.

6. Frederick Law Olmsted to Bertha Olmsted, January 28, 1862, *PFLO* 4:256.

7. Frederick Law Olmsted to the Board of Commissioners, January 22, 1861, *PFLO* 3:303.

8. Frederick Law Olmsted, *Walks and Talks of an American Farmer in England* (1852; repr., Amherst: University of Massachusetts Press, 2002), 145. See also Frederick Law Olmsted to the Board of Commissioners, May 20, 1858, *PFLO* 3:191. His punctuation is slightly altered in the board's version.

9. Samuel Parsons, "History of the Development of Central Park," *Proceedings of the New York State Historical Association* 17 (1919): 167. Parsons was assistant to Vaux from 1879 to 1884 and his partner from 1887 to 1895.

10. Frederick Law Olmsted to Calvert Vaux, June 8, 1865, *PFLO* 5:390.

11. Frederick Law Olmsted to Elizabeth Baldwin Whitney, December 16, 1890, *PFLO* 9:247–48.

12. Frederick Law Olmsted to Elizabeth Baldwin Whitney, December 16, 1890, *PFLO* 9:248.

13. Calvert Vaux to Frederick Law Olmsted, June 3, 1865, *PFLO* 5:383–88.

14. Frederick Law Olmsted, *The Spoils of the Park: With a Few Leaves from the Deep-Laden Note-Books of "A Wholly Unpractical Man"* (Detroit, MI: n.p., 1882), 23.

15. Frederick Law Olmsted to Charles Loring Brace, December 8, 1860, *PFLO* 3:286.

16. Katharine Prescott Wormeley, *The Other Side of War* (Boston: Ticknor and Company, 1889), 108.

17. Wormeley, *The Other Side of War*, 9–10, 64, 102.

14. Big Artwork of the Republic

1. Frederick Law Olmsted to John Olmsted, March 11, 1864, in *The Papers of Frederick Law Olmsted*, ed. Charles E. Beveridge (Charlottesville: University of Virginia Press, 2022), 5:688. Subsequent citations are abbreviated *PFLO*.

2. Frederick Law Olmsted to Mary Perkins Olmsted, August 12, 1863, *PFLO* 5:206. See also Eugene Kinkead, *Central Park, 1858–1995: The Birth, Decline, and Renewal of a National Treasure* (New York: Norton, 1990).

3. Calvert Vaux to Frederick Law Olmsted, June 3, 1865, *PFLO* 3:269. Spelling normalized.

4. Ezra Pound, "Canto LXXXI" (1940), in *The Cantos of Ezra Pound* (New York: New Directions, 1970); Kinkead, *Central Park, 1858–1995*.

5. *Frederick Law Olmsted: Landscape Architect, 1822–1903*, ed. Frederick Law Olmsted Jr. and Theodora Kimball, 2 vols. (1928). The full subtitle is "Central Park as a Work of Art and as a Great Municipal Enterprise." Volume 1 was published in 1922, on the centennial of Olmsted's birth. Both volumes are sometimes cited by their shortened half title, *Forty Years of Landscape Architecture*.

6. Frederick Law Olmsted to James T. Fields, October 21, 1860, *PFLO* 3:269.

7. Calvert Vaux to Frederick Law Olmsted, June 3, 1865, *PFLO* 5:385.

8. Calvert Vaux to Clarence C. Cook, June 6, 1865, quoted in Roy Rosenzweig and Elizabeth

Blackmar, *The Park and the People: A History of Central Park* (Ithaca, NY: Cornell University Press, 1992), 136.

9. Samuel Parsons, "History of the Development of Central Park," *Proceedings of the New York State Historical Association* 17 (1919): 169.

10. Laurie Olin, "Frederick Law Olmsted's Triumph," *Wall Street Journal*, October 5, 2022.

11. Jessica Sain-Baird, "How Central Park Keeps New York City Healthy," *Central Park Conservancy Magazine*, April 25, 2017.

12. Frederick Law Olmsted to Mariana Griswold Van Rensselaer, May 22, 1893, *PFLO* 9:623; italics added.

13. Frederick Law Olmsted, "To Gardeners" (1872), *PFLO* 6:538.

14. Ralph Waldo Emerson, "Love" (1841), in *Essays & Lectures*, ed. Joel Porte (New York: Library of America, 1983), 331. For his use of this quotation from Emerson, see Olmsted, "Mount Royal" (1881), *PFLO*, Supplemental Series 1:350.

15. See Jesse Green, "Review: Shakespeare's 'Merry Wives,' Now in South Harlem," *New York Times*, August 9, 2021.

16. Roberta Rampton, "What Happens When President Obama Takes a Stroll in Central Park," *Reuters*, July 18, 2015.

17. Harold Rosenberg, "Time and Space Concepts in Environmental Art" (1980), in *Art in the Land: A Critical Anthology of Environmental Art*, ed. Alan Sonfist (New York: Dutton, 1983), 204.

18. Ralph Waldo Emerson, *Nature* (1836), in *Essays & Lectures*, 9.

19. Christo, speaking in a documentary film directed by Albert Maysles, et al., *The Gates: The 26-Year Journey of Christo and Jeanne-Claude* (2007), Maysles Films, 138 minutes.

20. Clarence C. Cook, *A Description of the New York Central Park* (1869; repr., New York: New York University Press, 2017), 81. Cook had studied architecture with Andrew Downing at Newburgh, where he also worked with Vaux. He continued on close enough terms with Vaux that, during an illness, Cook would visit him twice daily.

21. Jordan Alexander Stein, "Fitz-Greene Halleck: The Most Famous Gay Poet You've Never Heard Of," Lecture The Library Company of Philadelphia, October 14, 2021.

22. See "Statues, Monuments & Ornamental Features," Central Park Conservancy, https://www.centralparknyc.org/locations?filters=statues-monuments-ornamental-features.

23. Frederick Law Olmsted to Elizabeth Baldwin Whitney, December 16, 1890, *PFLO* 9:247.

24. [Mariana Griswold] Van Rensselaer, *Art Out-of-Doors: Hints on Good Taste in Gardening* (New York: Charles Scribner's Sons, 1893), vii. In addition to corresponding extensively with Olmsted, Van Rensselaer published a biographical article about him in *The Century Illustrated Monthly Magazine* in October 1893.

25. Henry D. Thoreau, *Walden* (1854), ed. Jeffrey S. Cramer (New Haven, CT: Yale University Press, 2004), 125 ("Solitude").

15. Decline & Renewal

1. Frederick Law Olmsted to Henry Whitney Bellows, December 25, 1863, in *The Papers of Frederick Law Olmsted*, ed. Charles E. Beveridge (Charlottesville: University of Virginia Press, 2022), 5:165. Spelling normalized. Subsequent citations are abbreviated *PFLO*.

2. Frederick Law Olmsted to Mary Perkins Olmsted, October 15, [1863], *PFLO* 5:111.

3. Frederick Law Olmsted to John Olmsted, March 11, 1864, *PFLO*, 5.688.

4. On the failure of the Mariposa Company, see Laura Wood Roper, *FLO: A Biography of Frederick Law Olmsted* (Baltimore: Johns Hopkins University Press, 1973), 275–79.

5. Frederick Law Olmsted to Henry Whitney Bellows, August 16, 1863, *PFLO* 5:697.

6. Katharine Prescott Wormeley, *The Other Side of War* (Boston: Ticknor and Company, 1889), 63.

7. Frederick Law Olmsted to Frederick Newman Knapp, April 16, 1865, *PFLO* 5:354.

8. Calvert Vaux to Frederick Law Olmsted, May 10, 1865, *PFLO* 5:359.

9. Frederick Law Olmsted to Calvert Vaux, March 12, 1865, *PFLO* 5:324.

10. Frederick Law Olmsted, "Autobiographical Fragment B," in *Frederick Law Olmsted: Writings on Landscape, Culture, and Society*, ed. Charles E. Beveridge (New York: Library of America, 2015), 6. He quotes from "Tintern Abbey," among the multiple epigraphs to "Mount Royal" (1881), *PFLO*, Supplemental Series 1:350.

11. Frederick Law Olmsted to Charles Loring Brace, November 24, 1871, *PFLO* 6:493.

12. Samuel Parsons, "History of the Development of Central Park," *Proceedings of the New York State Historical Association* 17 (1919): 171–72.

13. Frederick Law Olmsted to Columbus Ryan, February 27, 1872, *PFLO* 6:523.

14. Frederick Law Olmsted, *The Spoils of the Park: With a Few Leaves from the Deep-Laden Note-Books of "A Wholly Unpractical Man"* (Detroit, MI: n.p., 1882), 36, 25, 48, 50.

15. Ralph Waldo Emerson, *Nature* (1836), in *Essays & Lectures*, ed. Joel Porte (New York: Library of America, 1983), 28 ("Discipline"). On an ethics of biocentrism, see Paul W. Taylor, *Respect for Nature: A Theory of Environmental Ethics* (Princeton, NJ: Princeton University Press, 1986).

16. René Descartes, *Discourse on the Method of Rightly Conducting One's Reason and of Seeking Truth in the Sciences* (1637), ed. and trans. Charles W. Eliot, Harvard Classics (New York: Collier, 1909–1914), part VI ("maîtres et possesseurs de la nature"). On the manager as a representative figure of modern failures in ethical thought and action, see Alasdair MacIntyre, *After Virtue: A Study in Moral Theory*, 3rd ed. (Notre Dame, IN: University of Notre Dame Press, 2007).

17. Nina Lakhani, "Emissions from Israel's War in Gaza Have 'Immense' Effect on Climate Catastrophe," *The Guardian*, January 9, 2024.

18. Walter Karp, "The Central Park," *American Heritage*, April/May 1981, https://www.americanheritage.com/central-park.

19. Fred Ferretti, "New York Parks Face a Touch-and-Go Summer," *New York Times*, May 26, 1977. The original article is slightly revised in the digital reprint, cited here.

20. Elizabeth Barlow Rogers, *Saving Central Park: A History and a Memoir* (New York: Knopf, 2018), ix.

21. See Gail Cornwall, "How Central Park Could Fix Public Education," *The Atlantic*, May 4, 2017. Cornwall offers striking before-and-after photos of the Great Lawn.

22. Elizabeth Barlow Rogers is principal author of a collection—packed with photos, diagrams, and data—entitled *Rebuilding Central Park: A Management and Restoration Plan* (Cambridge, MA: MIT Press, 1987).

23. Lisa W. Foderaro, "A $100 Million Thank-You for a Lifetime's Central Park Memories," *New York Times*, October 23, 2012.

24. Laura Paddison, "Ocean Water Is Rushing Miles Underneath the 'Doomsday Glacier' with Potentially Dire Impacts on Sea Level Rise," *CNN*, updated May 21, 2024.

25. John Podesta, "The Climate Crisis, Migration, and Refugees," Brookings Institution, July 25, 2019, https://www.brookings.edu/articles/the-climate-crisis-migration-and-refugees/;

Leslie Kaufman, "More Than 3 Million Americans Are Already Climate Migrants, Researchers Say," *Bloomberg*, December 18, 2023.

26. António Guterres, "Secretary-General's Video Message for Press Conference to Launch the Synthesis Report of the Intergovernmental Panel on Climate Change," United Nations, March 20, 2023.

27. "Climate Adaptation Project List," UN Environment Programme, https://www.unep.org/explore-topics/climate-action/what-we-do/climate-adaptation/climate-adaptation-project-list.

28. James Barron, "Near Flaco's Hunting Grounds, A Regreening of Central Park," *New York Times*, February 26, 2024.

29. Frederick Law Olmsted to Calvert Vaux, June 8, 1865, *PFLO* 5:390.

Conclusion

1. Frederick Law Olmsted to Mariana Griswold Van Rensselaer, June 11, 1893, in *The Papers of Frederick Law Olmsted*, ed. Charles E. Beveridge (Charlottesville: University of Virginia Press, 2022), 9:644. Subsequent citations are abbreviated *PFLO*.

2. Petteri Taalas, quoted in Damian Carrington, "Climate Limit of 1.5C Close to Being Broken, Scientists Warn," *The Guardian*, May 9, 2022.

3. Associated Press in Mexico City, "Monkeys 'Falling out of Trees like Apples' in Mexico Amid Brutal Heatwave," *The Guardian*, May 21, 2024.

4. See Clayton Page Aldern, *The Weight of Nature: How a Changing Climate Changes Our Brains* (New York: Dutton, 2024); and Robert Jisung Park, *Slow Burn: The Hidden Costs of a Warming World* (Princeton, NJ: Princeton University Press, 2024).

5. Committee on Statuary, Fountains, and Architecture to the Board of Commissioners, April 10, 1862, quoted in Roy Rosenzweig and Elizabeth Blackmar, *The Park and the People: A History of Central Park* (Ithaca, NY: Cornell University Press, 1992), 199.

6. Olmsted & Vaux, Landscape Architects, "Examination of the Design of the Park and of Recent Changes Therein," *PFLO* 1:257.

7. "Description of the Central Park" (1859), *PFLO* 3:213. Olmsted welcomes the vicious as well as the virtuous only "so far as each can partake therein without infringing upon the rights of others, and no further."

8. See, for example, Louise Dettman, "Following in Olmsted's Footsteps: Reimagining Public Places to Foster Health, Well-being," *Public Health News*, July 31, 2021; and John Olmsted, "The Design Principles of Frederick Law Olmsted in Light of Recent Psychological Research," Olmsted Network, March 23, 2023, https://olmsted.org/the-design-principles-of-frederick-law-olmsted-in-light-of-recent-psychological-research/.

9. David J. Nowak and Gordon M. Heisler, "Air Quality Effects of Urban Trees and Parks," National Recreation and Park Association, Research Series, 2010, https://www.nrpa.org/globalassets/research/nowak-heisler-research-paper.pdf.

10. Jessica Sain-Baird, "How Central Park Keeps New York City Healthy," *Central Park Conservancy Magazine*, April 25, 2017.

11. Joseph MacDonald, "How Cities Use Parks for Climate Change Management," American Planning Association, City Parks Forum Briefing Papers 11, February 1, 2007, https://www.planning.org/publications/document/9148693; Farshid Aram et al., "The Cooling Effect of Large-Scale Urban Parks on Surrounding Area Thermal Comfort," *Energies* 12, no. 20 (2019): 3904.

12. Frederick Law Olmsted, *Public Parks and the Enlargement of Towns* (1870; repr., New York: Arno Press, 1970), 67.

13. Geoffrey H. Donovan et al., "The Association between Tree Planting and Mortality: A Natural Experiment and Cost-Benefit Analysis," *Environment International* 170 (December 2022): 107609.

14. Jane E. Brody, "The Secret to Good Health May Be a Walk in the Park," *New York Times*, December 3, 2018. Brody quotes Adrian Benepe, senior vice president of the Trust for Public Land.

15. Lisa W. Foderaro and Will Klein, "Evidence: Parks Are Really Good for Mental, Physical, and Environmental Health," *The Power of Parks to Promote Health: A Special Report*, Trust for Public Land, May 24, 2023, https://www.tpl.org/parks-promote-health-report.

16. "Climate Change and Heat Islands," US Environmental Protection Agency, updated June 3, 2024, https://www.epa.gov/heatislands/climate-change-and-heat-islands.

17. "Cholera," World Health Organization, December 5, 2024, www.who.int/news-room/fact-sheets/detail/cholera.

18. Laura Wood Roper, *FLO: A Biography of Frederick Law Olmsted* (Baltimore: Johns Hopkins University Press, 1973), 61.

19. Scott Klein, "Infographics in the Time of Cholera," *ProPublica*, March 16, 2016.

20. Jennifer Harlan, "Overlooked No More: Emma Stebbins, Who Sculpted an Angel of New York," *New York Times*, May 29, 2019.

21. Gregory Gondwe, "Malawi Cholera Outbreak Death Toll Rises above 1,000," *AP*, January 25, 2023.

22. Stephanie Nolen, "Cholera Outbreaks Surge Worldwide as Vaccine Supply Drains," *New York Times*, updated November 1, 2022.

23. Jon Johnson, "How Long You Can Live without Water," *MedicalNewsToday*, May 14, 2019.

24. "Water and Climate Change," UN-Water, United Nations, https://www.unwater.org/water-facts/water-and-climate-change.

25. S. D. Fernando, "Climate Change and Malaria—A Complex Relationship," *UN Chronicle*, https://www.un.org/en/chronicle/article/climate-change-and-malaria-complex-relationship. See also Laurie Garrett, *The Coming Plague: Newly Emerging Diseases in a World Out of Balance* (New York: Farrar, Straus and Giroux, 1994).

26. Neil Vora, "'The Last of Us' Is Right. Our Warming Planet Is a Petri Dish," *New York Times*, April 2, 2023.

27. "Water and Climate Change," UN-Water, United Nations, https://www.unwater.org/water-facts/water-and-climate-change.

28. Fiona Harvey, "Water Scarcity on Agenda as Cop27 Climate Talks Enter Second Week," *The Guardian*, November 14, 2022; Fiona Harvey, "Global Fresh Water Demand Will Outstrip Supply by 40% by 2030, Say Experts," *The Guardian*, March 16, 2023.

29. "Our Journey," Peace Parks Foundation, https://www.peaceparks.org/about/our-journey.

30. Piers M. Forster et al., "Indicators of Global Climate Change 2023: Annual Update of Key Indicators of the State of the Climate System and Human Influence," *Earth System Science Data* 16, no. 6 (2024): 2625–58.

31. "The Central Park Climate Lab: Leading The Fight Against the Effects of Climate Change on City Parks," Central Park Conservancy, January 11, 2022, https://www.centralparknyc.org/press/climate-lab-leading-fight-against-climate-change-city-parks. The partnership also

includes the Natural Areas Conservancy, based in New York City. See also Chi-Ru Chang and Ming-Huang Li, "Effects of Urban Parks on the Local Urban Thermal Environment," *Urban Forestry & Urban Greening* 13, no. 4 (2014): 672–81.

32. Nadina Galle, *The Nature of Our Cities: Harnessing the Power of the Natural World to Survive a Changing Planet* (New York: Mariner Books, 2024), 32.

33. Ajit Niranjan, "Earth on Verge of Five Catastrophic Climate Tipping Points, Scientists Warn," *The Guardian*, December 5, 2023.

34. Roman Krznaric, *The Good Ancestor: A Radical Prescription for Long-Term Thinking* (New York: The Experiment, 2020), 14.

35. Rajiv Shah, *Big Bets: How Large-Scale Change Really Happens* (New York: Simon & Schuster, 2023). Shah was administrator of the US Agency for International Development (USAID) from 2010 to 2015.

36. Neta C. Crawford, "Pentagon Fuel Use, Climate Change, and the Costs of War," *Costs of War*, Watson Institute for International and Public Affairs, Brown University, updated November 13, 2019.

37. Rebecca Solnit, "Difficult Is Not the Same as Impossible," in *Not Too Late: Changing the Climate Story from Despair to Possibility*, ed. Rebecca Solnit and Thelma Young Lutunatabua (Chicago: Haymarket Books, 2023), 5. See also Solnit, *Hope in the Dark: Untold Histories, Wild Possibilities* (2004), 3rd ed. (Chicago: Haymarket Books, 2016).

38. Jonathan Lear, *Radical Hope: Ethics in the Face of Cultural Devastation* (Cambridge, MA: Harvard University Press, 2008), 135.

39. E. O. Wilson, *Half-Earth: Our Planet's Fight for Life* (New York: Norton, 2016), 209.

40. Goddard Digital Team, "NASA Data Shows July 22 Was Earth's Hottest Day on Record," NASA News & Events, July 29, 2024.

41. Tristan Roberts, "We Spend 90% of Our Time Indoors. Says Who?," *BuildingGreen*, https://www.buildinggreen.com/blog/we-spend-90-our-time-indoors-says-who.

42. "2024 Mid-Year Impact Report," New York Restoration Project, https://www.nyrp.org/en/2024-mid-year-impact-report.

43. "Benefits of Urban Parks," City Parks Alliance, https://cityparksalliance.org/about-us/why-city-parks-matter.

44. Henry D. Thoreau, *Walden* (1854), ed. Jeffrey S. Cramer (New Haven, CT: Yale University Press, 2004), 315 ("Conclusion").

INDEX

David Brown Morris, writer and scholar, retired as University Professor at the University of Virginia from a position split between English and the School of Medicine. His book *The Culture of Pain* (1991) won a PEN prize and led to multiple lectures and essays in pain medicine. It also initiates a trilogy that includes *Illness and Culture in the Postmodern Age* (1998) and *Eros and Illness* (2017). Earlier work includes two prizewinning books in eighteenth-century studies, *The Religious Sublime* (1972) and *Alexander Pope: The Genius of Sense* (1984). In addition to numerous essays and articles, he has written three books of narrative nonfiction: *Earth Warrior* (1995), about an anti-driftnet mission with environmental activist Paul Watson; *Civil War Duet* (2019), an intergenerational dialogue with his great-grandfather, Newton Brown, who served with the 101st Ohio Volunteer Infantry; and the wide-ranging *Wanderers: Literature, Culture and the Open Road* (2021). He held several distinguished professorships and has received yearlong grants from the Guggenheim Foundation, the National Endowment for the Humanities, the American Society of Learned Fellows, and (awarded jointly with NEH) the National Science Foundation.

SELECT TITLES FROM EMPIRE STATE EDITIONS

Daniel Campo, *The Accidental Playground: Brooklyn Waterfront Narratives of the Undesigned and Unplanned*

John Waldman, *Heartbeats in the Muck: The History, Sea Life, and Environment of New York Harbor, Revised Edition*

John Waldman (ed.), *Still the Same Hawk: Reflections on Nature and New York*

Joseph B. Raskin, *The Routes Not Taken: A Trip Through New York City's Unbuilt Subway System*

North Brother Island: The Last Unknown Place in New York City. Photographs by Christopher Payne, A History by Randall Mason, Essay by Robert Sullivan

Kirsten Jensen and Bartholomew F. Bland (eds.), *Industrial Sublime: Modernism and the Transformation of New York's Rivers, 1900–1940.* Introduction by Katherine Manthorne

Stephen Miller, *Walking New York: Reflections of American Writers from Walt Whitman to Teju Cole*

Tom Glynn, *Reading Publics: New York City's Public Libraries, 1754–1911*

Mark Naison and Bob Gumbs, *Before the Fires: An Oral History of African American Life in the Bronx from the 1930s to the 1960s*

Robert Weldon Whalen, *Murder, Inc., and the Moral Life: Gangsters and Gangbusters in La Guardia's New York*

Joanne Witty and Henrik Krogius, *Brooklyn Bridge Park: A Dying Waterfront Transformed*

Sharon Egretta Sutton, *When Ivory Towers Were Black: A Story about Race in America's Cities and Universities*

Pamela Hanlon, *A Wordly Affair: New York, the United Nations, and the Story Behind Their Unlikely Bond*

David J. Goodwin, *Left Bank of the Hudson: Jersey City and the Artists of 111 1st Street.* Foreword by DW Gibson

Nandini Bagchee, *Counter Institution: Activist Estates of the Lower East Side*

Susan Celia Greenfield (ed.), *Sacred Shelter: Thirteen Journeys of Homelessness and Healing*

Elizabeth Macaulay-Lewis and Matthew M. McGowan (eds.), *Classical New York: Discovering Greece and Rome in Gotham*

Colin Davey with Thomas A. Lesser, *The American Museum of Natural History and How It Got That Way*. Forewords by Neil deGrasse Tyson and Kermit Roosevelt III

Jim Mackin, *Notable New Yorkers of Manhattan's Upper West Side: Bloomingdale–Morningside Heights*

Matthew Spady, *The Neighborhood Manhattan Forgot: Audubon Park and the Families Who Shaped It*

Robert O. Binnewies, *Palisades: 100,000 Acres in 100 Years*

Marilyn S. Greenwald and Yun Li, *Eunice Hunton Carter: A Lifelong Fight for Social Justice*

Jeffrey A. Kroessler, *Sunnyside Gardens: Planning and Preservation in a Historic Garden Suburb*

Elizabeth Macaulay-Lewis, *Antiquity in Gotham: The Ancient Architecture of New York City*

Ron Howell, *King Al: How Sharpton Took the Throne*

Jean Arrington with Cynthia S. LaValle, *From Factories to Palaces: Architect Charles B. J. Snyder and the New York City Public Schools*. Foreword by Peg Breen

Boukary Sawadogo, *Africans in Harlem: An Untold New York Story*

Alvin Eng, *Our Laundry, Our Town: My Chinese American Life from Flushing to the Downtown Stage and Beyond*

Stephanie Azzarone, *Heaven on the Hudson: Mansions, Monuments, and Marvels of Riverside Park*

Ron Goldberg, *Boy with the Bullhorn: A Memoir and History of ACT UP New York*. Foreword by Dan Barry

Peter Quinn, *Cross Bronx: A Writing Life*

Mark Bulik, *Ambush at Central Park: When the IRA Came to New York*

Matt Dallos, *In the Adirondacks: Dispatches from the Largest Park in the Lower 48*

Brandon Dean Lamson, *Caged: A Teacher's Journey Through Rikers, or How I Beheaded the Minotaur*

Raj Tawney, *Colorful Palate: Savored Stories from a Mixed Life*

Edward Cahill, *Disorderly Men*

Joseph Heathcott, *Global Queens: An Urban Mosaic*

Francis R. Kowsky with Lucille Gordon, *Hell on Color, Sweet on Song: Jacob Wrey Mould and the Artful Beauty of Central Park*

Jill Jonnes, *South Bronx Rising: The Rise, Fall, and Resurrection of an American City, Third Edition*

Barbara G. Mensch, *A Falling-Off Place: The Transformation of Lower Manhattan*

David J. Goodwin, *Midnight Rambles: H. P. Lovecraft in Gotham*

Felipe Luciano, *Flesh and Spirit: Confessions of a Young Lord*

Jennifer Baum, *Just City: Growing Up on the Upper West Side When Housing Was a Human Right*

Davida Siwisa James, *Hamilton Heights and Sugar Hill: Alexander Hamilton's Old Harlem Neighborhood Through the Centuries*

Annik LaFarge, *On the High Line: The Definitive Guide, Third Edition.* Foreword by Rick Dark

Marie Carter, *Mortimer and the Witches: A History of Nineteenth-Century Fortune Tellers*

Alice Sparberg Alexiou, *Devil's Mile: The Rich, Gritty History of the Bowery.* Foreword by Peter Quinn

Carey Kasten and Brenna Moore, *Mutuality in El Barrio: Stories of the Little Sisters of the Assumption Family Health Service.* Foreword by Norma Benítez Sánchez

Kimberly A. Orcutt, *The American Art-Union: Utopia and Skepticism in the Antebellum Era*

Jonathan Butler, *Join the Conspiracy: How a Brooklyn Eccentric Got Lost on the Right, Infiltrated the Left, and Brought Down the Biggest Bombing Network in New York*

Nicole Gelinas, *Movement: New York's Long War to Take Back Its Streets from the Car*

Jack Hodgson, *Young Reds in the Big Apple: The New York Young Pioneers of America, 1923–1934*

Lynn Ellsworth, *Wonder City: How to Reclaim Human-Scale Urban Life*

Walter Zev Feldman, *From the Bronx to the Bosphorus: Klezmer and Other Displaced Musics of New York*

Larry Racioppo, *Here Down on Dark Earth: Loss and Remembrance in New York City*

Bonnie Yochelson, *Too Good to Get Married: The Life and Photographs of Miss Alice Austen*

Eve M. Kahn, *Queen of Bohemia Predicts Own Death: The Forgotten Journalist Zoe Anderson Norris, 1860-1914*

Miriam Chaiken, *Creative Ozone: The Artists of Westbeth*

Stefanie Mercado Altman, Claire Altman, and Stan Altman, *Twice Blessed: A Story of Unconditional Love.* Foreword by Stephen G. Post

Stephanie Azzarone, *Fabulous Fountains of New York*

For a complete list, visit www.fordhampress.com/empire-state-editions.